JUMPING FOR KIDS

JUMPING
FOR KIDS

Lesley Ward

Storey Publishing

The mission of Storey Publishing is to serve our customers by publishing practical information that encourages personal independence in harmony with the environment.

Edited by Lisa H. Hiley and Deborah Burns
Art direction by Mary Velgos
Cover design by Jen Rork
Text design and production by Jen Rork
Illustrations by Chuck Galey: 14, 28, 38, 42–43, 44, 68–69, 77, JoAnna Rissanen: 26, 41; Claudia Coleman: i; and Jim Dyekman: 18–19
Indexed by Susan Olason/Indexes and Knowledge Maps

The information in this book is true and complete to the best of our knowledge. All recommendations are made without guarantee on the part of the author or Storey Publishing. The author and publisher disclaim any liability in connection with the use of this information. For additional information please contact Storey Publishing, 210 MASS MoCA Way, North Adams, MA 01247.

Storey books are available for special premium and promotional uses and for customized editions. For further information, please call 1-800-793-9396.

Printed in China by Regent Publishing Services
10 9 8 7 6 5 4 3 2 1

Library of Congress Cataloging-in-Publication Data

Ward, Lesley.
Jumping for kids / by Lesley Ward.
    p. cm.
Includes index.
ISBN 13: 978-1-58017-672-9 (pbk. : alk. paper)
ISBN 13: 978-1-58017-671-2 (hardcover : alk. paper)
1. Jumping (Horsemanship) -- Juvenile literature. 2. Show jumping -- Juvenile literature. I. Title.
SF309.7.W37 2007
798.2'5—dc22   2006034466

Acknowledgments

I'd like to thank Megan Lynn, Alyssa Broner, Jessica Leonard, Emma Holland, Hannah Salyer, Marti Whitehouse, and all of the other talented young riders who appear in this book.

Contents

A Note to Parents

If you have a pony-mad child who rides English style, it's likely that she (or he!) has two main goals: to win a ribbon at a show and to learn how to jump. Young horse lovers are constantly dreaming about galloping toward a fence and leaping over it! It's amazing how quickly children learn how to ride. They can be so brave. One minute they're learning how to hold the reins, and the next minute they're cantering around the arena with a smile on their face. If most young riders had their way, they'd be jumping during their second or third lesson.

But jumping must be taught in a safe and structured way. Pointing a 1,000-pound horse at an obstacle and asking him to leap over it can be risky. Riders fall off more while jumping than while riding on the flat. That's why it's so important that *you* make sure your child's introduction to jumping is handled properly. If her early jumping experiences are positive, fun, and safe, she'll probably continue riding for life.

Be Involved

Even if you've never put a foot in a stirrup, it's essential that you carefully supervise your child's riding education. Your active involvement in your child's passion will help to ensure her safety. It's important that you learn as much as you can about horses and riding. Not only will this knowledge provide you with a better understanding of what your child is doing at the barn but also it will allow you to actively participate in her life, and what could be more wonderful than that?

So, it's up to you to make sure your child begins her jumping career on the right "hoof." In an ideal world, a child will have a wonderful trainer who will teach her how to jump a well-behaved pony over tiny fences and will guide her as she slowly graduates to bigger and more challenging obstacles. But in reality, good riding

Most young riders are eager to start jumping.

instruction is sometimes difficult to find, and it can also be challenging to find experienced horses and ponies for your child to ride. Although one of your top goals should be to find a good trainer, this book is intended to teach the basics of jumping to children who already have a solid foundation in the saddle. After reading it, she should be able to learn how, with your supervision, to pop over a fence safely.

Before you even think about letting your child jump, however, she must be able to walk, trot, and canter her horse by herself. She must be able to stop and steer and ride confidently in a group. And what about her horse? Does he know how to jump? If he is inexperienced, you need to sign both child and horse up for lessons with a good trainer. If your child doesn't have a mount, find a trainer with seasoned lesson horses.

Lessons Are Key

How do you find an experienced trainer? Anyone can put up a sign and declare "I'm a trainer!" but someone who knows a lot about horses isn't necessarily a good teacher, even if he or she advertises as one. Look for a certified instructor. While many patient, thorough, and experienced instructors may not be certified to teach, this is a good place to start. Certified instructors have gone through a training program to learn how to be good trainers. If you don't know of any trainers in your area, you could contact the American Riding Instructors Association (www.riding-instructor.com). ARIA tests trainers to make sure they follow safety practices and stick to high standards of teaching. You'll be in good hands if you sign up with an ARIA-certified trainer.

The United States Eventing Association (www.useventing.com) also has an Instructor's Certification Program. Riders and trainers in the program attend regular educational seminars where they learn safe and effective teaching methods for riders of every level.

Before learning to jump, your child must have a solid foundation in the saddle.

Other parents of horsey kids are also a good source of information about trainers. Before you sign up your child for jumping lessons, visit the trainer's barn and watch her give a few lessons. Is safety a priority? Young riders should always wear helmets and proper riding gear. They should learn how to jump in an enclosed arena, not a big field. The fences should be made of standards and poles, not junk found around the barn. And the students should be jumping fences that are appropriate heights for their riding levels. If fence poles are flying and students are falling off, continue your search for a trainer!

If your child doesn't have a horse, look for a trainer who can provide safe, quiet mounts. The horses should jump calmly and nicely, despite novice riders clinging to their manes and bouncing around in the saddle. It may take some time to find a suitable trainer and lesson barn for your child, but the extra effort will be worth it.

Be an Advocate

Once your child begins jumping, be cautious. She may complain about trotting over poles, poles, and more poles, but she must master poles before she points her pony at a fence. Once she's jumping, keep the jumps low and don't raise them until you feel sure your child is capable of jumping bigger fences. If you think a trainer is pushing your child or her horse too hard and asking them to jump fences that are too high, speak up! One bad fall can ruin riding for your child. Jumping should be fun. It is fun!

Read this book along with your child. She may be practicing her jumping position on the flat now, but it won't be long before she's jumping her first tiny course at a show. As her confidence grows, the fences may get bigger and bigger and, perhaps, one day she'll gallop around a solid cross-country course at a one-day event or compete in a Pony Club show jumping rally. No fence will be too high if your young rider learns the basics of jumping right from the start!

Make sure your child has the proper riding gear, including a helmet, whenever she rides.

A Note to Riders

Jumping a fence is one of the most exciting things you can do on horseback. It feels like flying! If you spend lots of time in the saddle, I'll bet that your riding goals include learning how to jump or improving your jumping skills. You may be interested in jumping at shows or learning to jump cross-country fences. Perhaps you want to teach your favorite horse how to jump. This book will help you.

Too often, we point our horse at a fence, give him a squeeze with our legs, and pray that he'll go over it. If you've been riding a while, you'll know this doesn't always work! Don't worry. This book will help you develop your jumping skills, so that you can help your horse when he jumps, not hinder him.

You'll start out by trotting over poles, move on to jumping single fences, and finish up by cantering confidently around show-jumping and cross-country courses. And if you don't have any jumps at your barn to practice over, this book will teach you how to make some.

So what are you waiting for? Grab your helmet and gloves, shorten your stirrups a hole or two, and pick up a canter. It's time to jump!

CHAPTER 1
Off to a
Flying Start

FOR MANY RIDERS, flying over a fence is one of the most enjoyable things about riding a horse or pony. It's a great feeling to approach a fence and have your horse jump it perfectly — and jumping an entire course of fences is both exciting and challenging.

Before you even think about urging your favorite horse toward a fence, though, it's important that you are a confident, capable rider who can walk, trot, and canter both in and out of an arena. Why? Because jumping takes balance and a good seat. If you're not 100 percent secure in the saddle when your horse leaps into the air, you can make it difficult for him to jump and you could fall off. You must have complete control on the flat before you jump.

This means that before you start jumping, you must spend loads of time working on the flat with a trusted horse or pony. You need to know him inside and out before you begin popping over fences.

You need to know what signal or aid it takes to ask him to trot or canter, and you must know how much rein pressure is needed to slow him down or to turn him. If you can't stop your horse without yanking on the reins with all of your strength, maybe you shouldn't be jumping him quite yet.

Doing lots of flatwork will make both you and your horse better jumpers.

You also need to have "quiet hands" when you jump. Practice keeping your hands low and near to your horse's withers. If your hands fly around when you're trotting or cantering, grab hold of some mane or make sure your pinkies are touching your horse's mane.

Ask yourself if you can do the following with your horse. Be honest!

- Slow down and speed up instantly
- Stop easily
- Turn smoothly
- Control him in a group of horses

And what about you? Are you fit and ready to jump? How strong are your legs? Can you ride without stirrups for five or ten minutes around the arena? Can you rise to the trot without stirrups? You need to be fit and strong before you jump. Spending hours in the saddle will build up the muscles you need to jump.

When you are first learning to jump, you will probably start slowly. It may seem boring to spend several lessons trotting over poles on the ground, but doing this prepares you for jumping 3-foot fences later on.

Lessons, Lessons, Lessons!

Everyone needs lessons — even Olympic riders have coaches who help them on a regular basis. If you take regular lessons, your trainer will help you prepare for jumping. She'll make sure you can walk, trot, and canter with confidence and steer your horse properly. She'll help you improve your riding position and work on your aids. And when it's time to jump, she should make sure you begin in a safe way.

If you have your own horse and you don't take regular lessons, you should! It can be tough to become a better rider on your own. We all need someone to critique our riding position and help us when we can't figure out how to ask our horses to do something.

Also, it can be difficult to come up with interesting exercises to do during schooling sessions with our horses. Don't get stuck in a rut — just going round and round in circles is boring for both you and your horse. Talk to your parents about finding a good trainer and once you find one, try to schedule at least one lesson a week.

Lessons can be expensive, so think of ways that you can help pay for them. If you're old enough, you can babysit for younger children. You can offer to do yard work for your neighbors or care for their pets when they go on vacation. Some barns let you work off part of your lesson fees. You might clean tack or lead younger students during their lessons, for example, in exchange for reduced lesson fees or free lessons.

Finding a Trainer

Where can you find a trainer? Your local tack shop is a good place to start. Look on the bulletin board for trainer advertisements or cards. Ask the shop employees if they know of a great local trainer. Pick up any free horse magazines or other animal publications that you see and look at trainer ads. There might be a qualified

Trotting over poles on the ground prepares you for bigger jumps.

trainer who lives in your area. Visit local barns with your parents. Look for a barn that has lots of young riders and check out the instructors. While you're there, have a look around the barn to make sure the horses are well cared for and the facility is clean and safe.

Look for a trainer who has spent many years training horses and riders. If you want to compete in jumper classes, you might look for a trainer who competes in this division or who has students competing in this division. If you want to event, look for a trainer who competes herself or who takes students to events on a regular basis.

The best way to find a good trainer to teach you or your horse how to jump is to ask your pony pals who they ride with. If they give a trainer the thumbs up, you and your parents should watch a few lessons to see if you'd like to ride with that trainer, too. A good trainer won't mind you watching her give a lesson.

Attributes of a Good Trainer:

- She's patient and encourages her students.

- She pays equal attention to all of her students. She doesn't talk to other people when she's teaching a lesson.

- She teaches the entire time. If a lesson is 45 minutes, it lasts 45 minutes.

- She is a problem solver. If a student is having trouble getting her horse over a fence, a good trainer will spend time figuring out how to get the horse to jump without upsetting the horse or rider.

- She is kind to horses. She doesn't lose her temper and whip a horse.

- She teaches in an enclosed area and uses safe jumps.

- She wears a safety helmet with a chinstrap when she rides and jumps, and she insists her students do, too.

If you keep your horse at home, you may have to load him in a trailer and take him to a trainer's barn for a lesson. If you don't have a trailer, you might be able to find a trainer who will come to your farm to teach you. Her lesson fee may be a bit more expensive though, because she will have traveling expenses.

If there's a Pony Club in your area, sign up. Pony Club organizes regular group lessons for its members. These lessons are inexpensive and the Pony Club makes sure it uses good trainers.

If you join the Pony Club, you'll also be able to attend summer camps or "rallies" with your horse. At the rallies, you'll get to ride once or twice a day, and you'll spend time in unmounted classes where you'll learn about horse care and horse health.

Jumping Gear

Your regular riding clothes are fine for jumping. You must always wear a safety helmet, and gloves will help you grip the reins. Pull on a pair of jodhpurs or breeches to prevent nasty leg rubs, and wear boots with low heels to keep your feet in the stirrups.

It's also a good idea to wear a padded safety vest, like those worn by eventers and jockeys, because it helps prevent bruises and broken bones if you take a tumble.

And because riders may fall off when learning to jump, riding in safety stirrups with rubber bands on one side, called "peacock stirrups," is smart because they prevent you from being dragged by your horse if you "eat dirt."

Your horse's tack doesn't change much for jumping, but it's a good idea to put splint boots on all four of his legs. These are padded boots that you secure with Velcro fastenings. They protect your horse's legs if he kicks himself by mistake or hits a pole.

Before jumping, put splint boots on your horse to protect his legs.

Stay Safe by Using Protective Riding Gear

A. Boots protect your and your horse's legs. **B.** A safety vest protects you in a fall. Gloves help you grip the reins. **C.** A safety helmet with a chinstrap is a must! **D.** Safety stirrups can prevent you from being dragged.

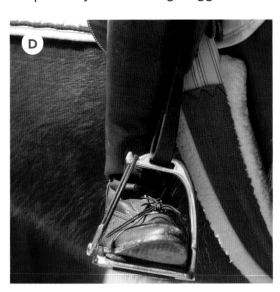

Shorten Your Stirrups

Once you and your horse are properly equipped, the first thing to do when learning how to jump is to shorten your stirrups. Shorter stirrups help bring your body weight forward so that you can stay over your horse's center of balance throughout the jump. This makes jumping a lot easier for both of you.

Shorter stirrups also help you push your heels down, making you more secure in the saddle, and they prevent you from sitting too far back, which can throw your horse off balance and cause him to knock down a pole with one of his feet.

The safest way to shorten your stirrups is from the ground before you get on your horse. Most people raise their stirrups about two holes when jumping. You can also shorten your stirrups when you are on your horse, but don't try this unless he's very well behaved and stands quietly when you ask him to halt. You will only have one hand on the reins while you shorten the stirrups, so your horse must be obedient.

To shorten your stirrups from the saddle, hold the reins in one hand to keep control. Leave your feet in the stirrups and adjust the leathers one at a time, holding your leg slightly away from the saddle.

You can shorten your stirrups while sitting in the saddle.

Jumping Position

Now it's time to practice jumping position, which is also called "two-point position," "forward position," or "half-seat." Lean forward over your horse's neck and lift your rear end slightly out of the saddle. Sitting forward like this helps you stay balanced and allows you to move with your horse as he jumps over a fence.

Jumping position makes it easier for your horse to leap over a fence because you're not bouncing around on his back or pulling on the reins, which he might think is a signal to halt. Let's take a look at a good jumping position.

Head: Look straight ahead; looking down affects your balance.

Shoulders: Keep your shoulders back and down.

Upper body: Lean your upper body forward over your horse's neck. Bend from your hips, not your waist. Stick your chest out a bit so that your back is flat and straight, not rounded and hunched over.

Seat: Push your rear end backward and lift it slightly out of the saddle. It should be close enough to the saddle that you can quickly and smoothly sit back into your regular riding position after you land.

Thighs: Your thighs should be close to the saddle.

Jumping position helps you stay balanced over a fence.

Lower legs: Keep your lower legs close to the girth, not stuck out in front of you. You should be able to feel your horse's sides with your calves. Keep your legs glued in this position even when you're flying over a fence. Don't grip with your knees and tip forward, because your lower legs will fly backward and you'll lose your balance.

Ankles: Let your ankles be flexible. They act as shock absorbers for the rest of your body and stop you from bumping around on your horse's back.

Feet: Place the ball of your foot (the widest part) on the stirrup pad and push your heels down lower than your toes. Remember — heels down at all times! It's okay if your toes turn out a little.

Arms: Push your arms forward so that your elbows are slightly in front of your body, not stuck by your sides as they are when you ride on the flat. Bend your arms at the elbow and imagine a straight line from your elbows all the way along your arms and through the reins to your horse's mouth, just as when you are in your regular riding position.

Hands: Keep your hands level and close to your horse's neck, with your thumbs facing upward. Close your fingers around the reins so they don't slip out of your hands. Keep your hands and arms soft, not stiff, so you can follow the motion of your horse's head and neck. If you feel a bit stiff, flap your elbows (like a bird!) a few times to loosen up.

Make Your Own Neck Strap

You can use a stirrup leather fastened around your horse's neck like a collar, but make sure it's not too tight. You might need to trim off some extra leather and add a few extra holes before it fits your horse properly.

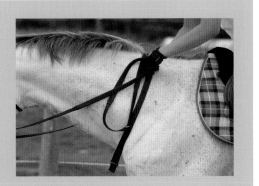

A Quick History of Jumping

THOUSANDS OF YEARS AGO when humans domesticated horses, it's likely they leaped over a log or two while they galloped around bareback, hunting for food. Years later, hunting became a sport for English gentlemen. Rich landowners galloped around the countryside in hot pursuit of deer or foxes.

In the mid-1700s, a law was passed in England that allowed landowners to enclose their fields with fences and hedges. When the hunters approached a fence or a hedge they had two choices: find a gate to go through or jump the obstacle! Most chose to jump. Jumping or "horse leaping" became a popular pastime and made hunting even more exciting.

In the 1800s and early 1900s, horses had to learn how to jump because soldiers rode them during wartime. Cavalry steeds were expected to jump huge fences and hedgerows during battles as their riders chased their enemies.

It's amazing that these horses made it over anything, because until the late 1800s, riders kept their bottoms in the saddle, lifted up their hands, and leaned back over the jumps. This style wasn't very comfortable for the rider and it made jumping more difficult for his poor horse!

Then along came Frederico Caprilli, a captain in the Italian cavalry and the chief riding instructor at the Italian Cavalry School at Pinerolo. He replaced the double bridles that cavalry horses were used to wearing with snaffle bridles.

He shortened his soldiers' stirrups and taught them to push down their heels and lean forward, over their horses' center of balance, when they jumped. He encouraged his men to move their hands forward and follow their horses' movement with the reins instead of jerking their horses' mouths.

This new position became known as the "forward seat" and that's how people jump today!

Practice on the Flat

Practice the jumping position at the walk, trot, and canter every time you ride. Stay in the position for a few minutes, then sit down and give yourself a short rest. Keep at it until you can hold it several times around the ring. Jumping position is tiring because you give your leg muscles a workout, but it is the best way to build balance and strength in the saddle.

If you have trouble staying in jumping position at first, grab hold of your horse's mane to stop you from falling back into the saddle. You could also put a neck strap on your horse and hold on to it. If you lose your balance while jumping, it's better to hang on to some mane or a neck strap than to yank on the reins or fall off. Your hands will stay still and you won't jerk your horse in the mouth with the bit, which is painful for him. If you pull on your horse's mouth a lot, he may not want to jump. As you become a more experienced and stronger jumper, you'll be able to stay in jumping position without these aids.

Practice the jumping position at the walk, trot, and canter.

Loosen your reins slightly over a fence so you don't jab your horse in the mouth.

The Release

As your horse leaps over a fence, he stretches out his head and neck. If you keep your hands glued to his withers, the reins will tighten and you'll jab him in the mouth. This confuses your horse. You're asking him to jump, but you're also putting pressure on his mouth, which tells him to stop. When you jump, it's important to temporarily loosen your hold on the reins and your horse's mouth. This is called a "crest release," because you rest your hands on the crest of your horse's neck. This is something you can practice at the walk or trot.

As you prepare to take off in front of a fence, push your hands forward, about 8 to 10 inches in front of the saddle. This loosens the reins slightly and allows your horse to stretch out his neck over the fence. To keep your hands still, you might want to hold on to some mane.

Trotting Poles

It's best to start out low when you learn to jump. How low? Poles-on-the-ground low! Trotting over a line of poles helps you practice your jumping position and improve your balance. Use white or colored trotting poles. If you don't have any poles, go to a home improvement store and buy a few 8-foot landscaping poles. Paint them black and white so that your horse can see them on the ground.

Use at least four or five trotting poles and place them parallel to each other, the correct distance apart. They should to be closer together if you're riding a short-striding pony and farther apart if you're riding a long-striding horse, because you don't want your mount to stumble over them.

Practice the jumping position over a line of trotting poles.

Practicing Over Poles

Once the poles are set, ask your horse to trot around the arena or field at a steady, active pace. He should feel bouncy and have a spring in his step; this is known as "impulsion," and your horse needs it to jump over a fence. If he's slopping along like a snail, he'll trip over the poles. If he's a bit sluggish, squeeze him with your legs every time you rise out of the saddle, or give him a quick nudge with your heels or a tap with the crop behind your leg.

A horse who's moving too quickly, though, might step on the poles instead of between them. If he's going too fast, sit down and post slowly through the poles. Squeeze the reins with your fingers to ask him to slow down.

Give yourself plenty of room to approach the poles in a straight line. Don't just yank your horse into them at the last second. Steer him toward the middle of the poles and, about two or three strides away from the first one, shift into jumping position. Push your hands forward slightly so you don't pull on his mouth. Here are some other things to think about as you trot over the poles:

- Keep your horse at a steady pace.
- Stay in the middle of the poles by keeping your reins even. If your horse veers to one side, press the same side rein on his neck and use your same side leg at the girth to push him back into the middle.
- Look straight ahead. Focus on the arena fence or a tree in the distance.
- Trot over the poles in both directions so you don't bore your horse to death.

After you've trotted over the last pole, sit back in the saddle and start posting again. Bring your hands back to their original position near the withers and take up

Trotting Pole Guide

PONY POLES:

Place them
3½–4 feet apart

HORSE POLES:

Place them
4½–5 feet apart

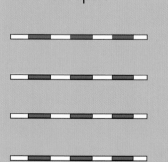

contact again with the reins. Keep your horse trotting after he finishes the poles. Some horses are lazy and will slow down to a walk after they trot over the last pole if you don't keep them working.

Practice with trotting poles for a week or so, or in several lessons with your instructor, until you are comfortable trotting over them. Then it's time to start jumping!

Always trot all the way through the line of poles.

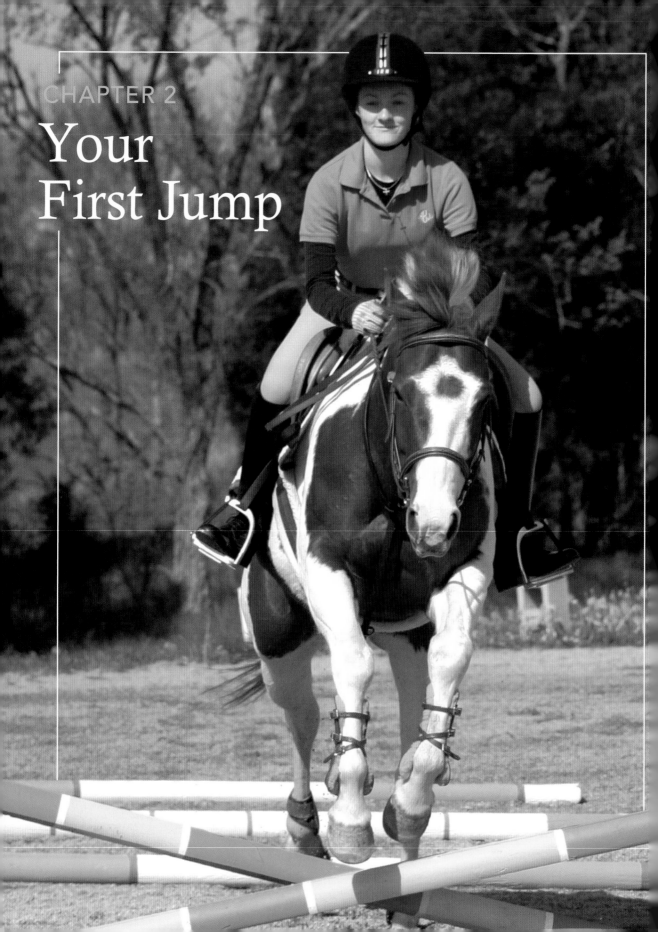

CHAPTER 2

Your First Jump

CREST RELEASE: A maneuver in which the rider moves her hands slightly up the horse's neck during a jump.

CROSS-RAIL: A fence made of two poles crossed between two standards.

GROUND POLE: A pole placed just in front of the vertical elements of a jump.

BEFORE YOU EVEN THINK about pointing your favorite horse at your first jump, you need to decide if he's up for the job. Is he an experienced horse who will jump anything in front of him, or is he a "greenie" who has never jumped a fence before? If you're just learning how to pop over fences yourself, it's really important that the horse you ride knows how to jump.

If you haven't been riding for very long, you need a "packer," a horse who will jump a fence even if you're just hanging on and not giving him the exactly correct signals. Riding a horse who will jump anything will build your confidence and make jumping even more fun. And you'll learn how to jump more quickly on an experienced horse.

An inexperienced rider plus an inexperienced horse equals trouble. If your greenie refuses a fence or knocks down poles, you won't know how to fix the problem and his behavior could get worse. He might hit his leg on a pole and get scared and buck. He might run away from the jumps.

If your horse is green, it's best to let a more experienced rider or trainer teach him how to jump before you attempt to fly over any fences with him. What should you do while he's being trained? Sign up for some lessons at a good barn on an experienced lesson horse. You may have to take a few flat lessons before you are allowed to jump, so the trainer can find out how well you ride. Be patient, you'll start jumping eventually.

What's a Fence?

A SIMPLE FENCE is usually made up of two sides, called "standards," which hold up a pole. Standards can be wide and look like a gate, or they can be made out of a 4×4 piece of wood. Some jump standards are made out of plastic.

Typical standards have holes in them for the jump cups, which are metal or plastic holders that attach to the standards with metal pins through the holes. The holes usually start at 1 foot and then go up in 3-inch increments. This allows you to set up a jump at 1 foot, 1 foot 3 inches, 1 foot 6 inches, and so on.

The poles that make up a fence are usually rounded and are 10 to 12 feet long. We'll show you how to make your own fences in chapter 5.

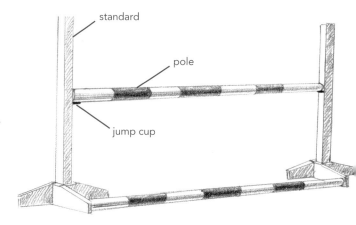

A *vertical* is a single pole. It can be difficult for a horse to judge the depth of the jump, so a ground pole helps him see where to take off.

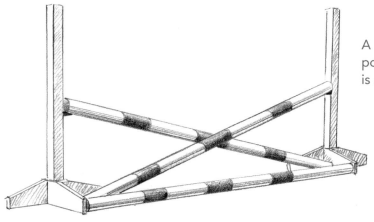

A *cross-rail* consists of two poles crossed in the middle and is a good fence for beginners.

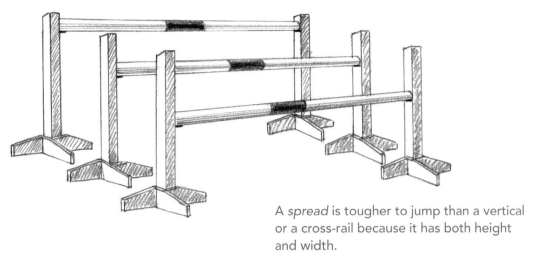

A *spread* is tougher to jump than a vertical or a cross-rail because it has both height and width.

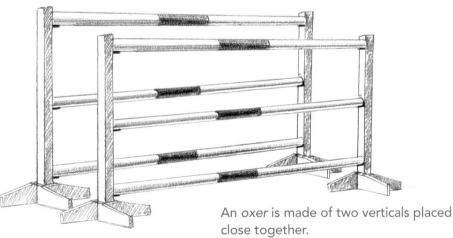

An *oxer* is made of two verticals placed close together.

A *rolltop* is a solid, rounded jump that is often covered with "grass" carpeting.

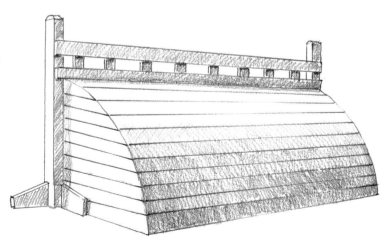

Starting Small

Once you're riding an experienced horse, you can aim for your first fence. To make sure you have a wonderful (and safe!) first jump, set up a small cross-rail fence at the end of a line of trotting poles. A cross-rail fence is made up of two poles that are crossed between two standards. One end of each pole rests in a jump cup and the other end of the pole lies on the ground.

The cross-rail fence should be about 9 feet away from the last pole. Keep the fence small — about 18 inches off the ground. It may seem tiny, but it's best to start small and work your way up.

It's important to put the trotting poles in front of the cross-rail fence because your horse should already be trained to trot over them at a nice, bouncy pace. Then jumping a fence at the end of the poles will be easy for him. As you head toward the poles, remember the following steps:

- Get into jumping position.
- Push your hands forward.
- Grab some mane.
- Push your heels down and keep your lower legs close to your horse's sides.
- Look straight ahead — over the cross-rail — and trot over the middle of the poles.

As you trot over the last pole, stay in jumping position and steer your horse into the middle of the cross-rail. If he feels pokey, squeeze him with your calves and then hang on. Since the fence is small, you shouldn't be thrown out of the saddle.

Once your horse lands, sit back gently and ask him to trot forward. Don't let him slow down or turn. Start rising to the trot again. Hooray — you jumped your first fence!

Your first jump should be a small cross-rail fence set up at the end of a line of trotting poles.

Do this exercise three or four times and then give your horse a break. While he's resting, ask your helper to raise the cross-rail an inch or two and trot over it a few more times. If your horse jumps nicely, your helper can change the cross-rail to a small vertical fence. Place one pole about 2 feet off the ground between the jump standards and put a second pole on the ground about 8 to 10 inches away from the fence.

The ground pole, sometimes called a ground line, makes a fence look more solid and helps a horse figure out where he should take off. Ride the exercise just like you did when it was a cross-rail at the end. Your horse should take the vertical easily.

Once you've mastered the cross-rail fence, set up a small vertical at the end of the line of trotting poles and jump it.

Five Phases of Jumping

To become a great jumper, you need to know the five phases of jumping — the approach, the take-off, the moment of suspension, the landing, and the getaway — and learn to perfect each stage. The actual jump may be the most exciting, but the other parts of a jump are equally important, so be sure to work on all the phases together.

Phase One: The Approach

As you head toward the fence, your horse must be balanced and going forward with lots of impulsion and rhythm. Aim right for the middle of the fence. Keep your heels down and maintain contact with your horse's mouth. Don't get in jumping position quite yet — your seat should brush the saddle lightly.

Phase Two: The Take-Off

Just before your horse takes off, he prepares himself for the leap by lowering and lengthening his neck. As he takes off, he rebalances himself by shortening his neck and lifting up his head. A willing, athletic horse tucks his forelegs up neatly while his hocks provide the power over the jump.

Follow your horse's movement by leaning forward from your hips and lifting your seat out of the saddle. Keep your back flat and your head up, looking forward.

Phase Three: The Moment of Suspension

When your horse is in midair, he should make a rounded shape, known as a bascule. To do this, he must arch his back, tuck all four legs up close to his body, and stretch out his head and neck. Your body should stay forward until your horse's hind legs have passed over the highest part of the jump.

Phase Four: The Landing

As your horse straightens his forelegs to land, he raises his head to balance himself. A horse must be supple and athletic to make a good landing and bring his hind legs through for phase five, the getaway. Sit back in the saddle gently, sit up tall, and ride forward in a straight line. Try not to land in the saddle with a big bump, because this can unbalance your horse.

Phase Five: The Getaway

In the getaway stride, your horse's hocks should come well under him to keep him balanced. If you're jumping a course, you should already be thinking about the next fence, so it's important that your horse be moving forward with energy, not poking along with his head on the ground. You should be sitting down in the saddle and be asking him to move forward by squeezing him with your lower legs.

Jumping a Single Fence

Once you've mastered the cross-rail at the end of trotting poles, it's time to try a single fence. Set up a simple vertical by itself in the arena. It may be hard to get your horse moving forward in a steady, active pace without the trotting poles to help you along, so give him a few squeezes with your lower legs before you head toward the fence, and circle once or twice to give yourself time to establish an energetic, bouncy pace. Then aim for the center of the fence.

Rise into jumping position a few feet out and grab hold of some mane or a neck strap so you loosen your hold on the reins slightly. Push your heels down, keep your lower legs on your horse's sides, and look up! If your horse begins to canter a few feet away from the jump, don't worry about it as long as he's cool and calm. Let him go forward and follow along with your body. But if he's racing at the fence and you feel that he's out of control, bring him back to a trot by sitting down in the saddle and posting. Then get back up in jumping position right in front of the fence. If you're far enough away from the fence that you can circle, go ahead and circle a few times to

If your horse is racing towards a fence, circle him a few times to slow him down and then approach it again.

calm him down and approach the fence again. Never pull on the reins right in front of a fence — you want your horse to think "forward," not "stop!"

As your horse is landing, keep your legs on his sides but don't squeeze him forward unless he really slows down. You'll be thrown back into the saddle as he reaches the ground, so use your legs to sit down gently and bring him back down to the trot if he's cantering. After you land, aim straight ahead.

Once you're a good distance away from the jump, turn right or left and continue round the arena or field. Alternate the direction you head in so you keep your horse thinking at all times. You could also ask him to halt, turn round, and approach the fence from the other direction. If you do this, make sure there's a ground pole on the other side of the fence as well.

Most horses jump smoothly if they take off about 3 feet away from the base of the fence. Experienced horses can usually figure this out for themselves, but an unbalanced rider can throw a horse off and make him take off too late or too soon. This is why it's important to get in jumping position and stay as still as you can.

If a horse takes off too early, he'll make a huge jump in the air and you could get left behind. This means you lose your balance and fall back into the saddle, banging your horse on the back and jerking him in the mouth. If a horse takes off too close to the fence, he'll put in a tiny extra stride, called "chipping," and pop over it awkwardly, which could cause him to knock down a pole with his front feet or might push you right out of the saddle.

If you lose your balance when jumping, you might get left behind.

Young or inexperienced horses often over-jump a fence.

The Half-Halt

As you become a more experienced rider, you'll learn how to adjust your horse's strides and his speed so he takes off at the right spot most of the time. When you're just learning how to jump, there are a few things you can do to adjust your horse's stride. If you're trotting toward a fence and your horse is being too speedy, slow down your posting. Instead of rising and sitting quickly, relax and think "slow down," and your horse may follow your lead. If you're cantering, you can try to slow him down by sitting more deeply in the saddle. Sit up straight, press your seat into the saddle, and say "whoa" in a calm voice.

More advanced riders often use half-halts to slow a horse down and to ask him to take more strides in front of a fence. A half-halt is what its name says, half a halt. You're not asking your horse to stop completely, just to slow down a bit and rebalance himself. A half-halt should make your horse more collected and bring his hocks underneath him. He should become springier and have more impulsion — just what you want for jumping!

Ask for a half-halt by sitting deeply in the saddle, closing your lower legs and pushing your horse forward into a "restraining hand." This means squeezing the reins firmly and keeping a strong contact.

Once your horse brings his hind legs underneath him and becomes more collected, you can lighten your seat and again follow your horse's head with your hands.

Jumping a Spread Fence

Once you are comfortable going over a vertical fence, set up a spread. This is a jump with two (a double bar) or three poles (a triple bar) set parallel to each other at different heights. It's made up of four or six jump standards, supporting two or three poles. Start with two pairs of standards, setting one pair behind the other. Keep them fairly close — you don't want your first spread fence to be too wide! Because a spread is wider than a vertical jump, your horse will spend more time in the air, so practice on a smaller fence first.

Put a pole on the ground at the base of the jump, around 3 to 5 inches in front of the raised pole. This ground pole, or ground line, makes the jump seem more solid and your horse will jump it more easily. The pole on the first set of standards should be about 2 feet off the ground. The pole on the second pair of standards should be about 2 feet 3 inches. Now you have an easy spread fence.

A horse spends more time in the air over a spread fence.

Aim for the middle of both fences when jumping a line.

Jumping Lines at the Trot

After you've mastered jumping a single fence, you can try a line. A line is two or more fences set up so your horse takes a specific number of strides between them. To begin with, set up two cross-rails about 60 feet apart. The large space between the two fences gives you time to land after the first fence, regain control of your horse, and aim him for the × of the second fence. Stay in the middle of the two fences and don't wiggle from side to side. Jump the line from both directions two or three times.

Trotting a Small Course

An easy trotting course is made up of single fences and lines. Jumping a course is a challenge because you have to memorize the order of fences and, as you approach each fence, you must think about where the next fence is and how you are going to approach that one. You must also concentrate on keeping the same pace throughout the course.

Ask your trainer or an experienced horse person to set up a course of seven or eight fences. An easy course to start with is two outside lines and two diagonal jumps set up in a figure eight. (See diagram, left.)

Pick up the trot and do a large circle to establish your pace, then head for the first fence. Get into jumping position in front of the fence, release the reins slightly, and hang on! Sit back down when your horse lands and rise to the trot again as you head toward fence number two. After you jump the last fence, make another circle and slow your horse down to a walk. This is a good habit to get into because you might need to make these circles when you jump in a show.

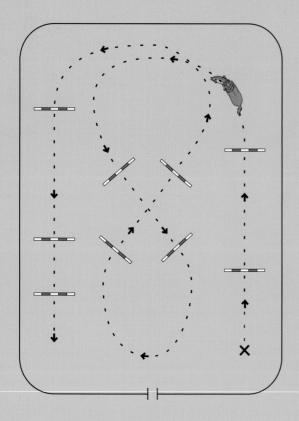

A Simple Trotting Course

Here is an example of a simple trotting course that your trainer could set up for you. Practice jumping any course from both directions — it's like having two courses instead of one!

Cantering Fences

Once you feel comfortable jumping at the trot, it's time to move up to the canter. The easiest way to learn how to canter fences is to jump a line. For a horse, set up the line with the jumps 60 or 72 feet apart. If you ride a pony, set up the jumps 40 or 51 feet apart. This will allow your horse or pony the same number of strides (the length or distance he travels with each step) each time he canters through the line. The average horse's stride is about 12 feet, so if a line is 60 feet long, he should jump it easily in five strides.

Trot into the first fence and ask your horse to canter after he lands. Many horses like to pick up the canter after they land, so this won't be hard. Squeeze with your lower legs to keep your horse cantering while you look over the second fence. Try to keep your horse at the same speed by keeping a firm hold on the reins and then get into jumping position in front of the jump. Push your hands forward to release your hold on the reins and then jump!

Trot into the first fence of a line and let your horse canter over the second.

Once you've mastered cantering between the two fences and over the last fence, you can try cantering toward the first fence of the line and then continue cantering until you've cleared the second fence. After that, canter over some single fences that are not part of a line. If your horse starts speeding up or jumping badly, you need to go back to trotting over some small fences until you feel like you are back in control. If your horse pops over the fences nicely, you can move on to cantering around a small course. But before you can do that, you should be able to establish a rhythm and count strides.

Establish a steady rhythm on the flat before you begin jumping.

Establishing Rhythm

Rhythm can be confusing, but it is very important when you're jumping. Think of rhythm like the drumbeat in a song. The main beat is steady and constant — it doesn't change. If you were to hear that song on a CD boom box that had really old batteries, the song would slow down and sound draggy. If there were fresh batteries in the boom box, it would play the song pretty quickly. But the tempo of the drums stays regular, just a little slower or faster depending on the batteries. It's like that when jumping. You can be zipping along at nearly a gallop, or you can be cantering collected and quiet, but the rhythm of your canter should stay matched, stride for stride.

To keep your horse on a rhythm, set out a couple of poles on the ground with several strides in between (you can decide, but five or six is good) and canter over them, counting out loud. Say "one-two, one-two" as you go along. Don't make your horse speed up or slow down just to fit the strides in — if you keep to that rhythm, you'll find that you can go over the poles perfectly, without hitting them or stretching to make that last one.

Count one-two, one-two, as you canter between two poles.

Counting Strides

Most courses are set up for an average horse's regular canter stride, which is about 12 feet long. Course designers want riders to complete all the jumps in a regular rhythm, which means cantering around and jumping at about the same speed all the way through, not speeding up here and slowing down there.

Strides are very important when it comes to jumping lines. If you canter too fast in between the jumps, you might get that awkward hopping step, or chip, right before the fence. Or you might leave out a stride altogether and jump from too long a spot, which could knock a rail down. If you canter too many strides between fences, you may be putting your horse too deep (close to the jump), and he may jump awkwardly, or even refuse. Cantering with a nice beat all the way around will make the course ride much easier.

Let's say you have a jumping line of two fences with five strides in between. How do you calculate the distance between the jumps to accommodate five strides?

Count strides with your trainer as you walk a jumping course.

Count the 5 strides at 12 feet each (5 × 12 = 60 feet) and then add a half stride (6 feet) for where the horse lands and where he takes off (2 × 6 = 12). The distance between the jumps is 72 feet. But even if you don't care about the actual measurement, you should still learn how to count strides on foot, by walking the course.

Except for people with very long legs, most of us take extra big strides when measuring distances. Don't take tiny steps — your stride should be about 3 feet long. Four of your big steps should equal approximately one horse stride. When walking a line, take one big stride away from the fence (that's your horse's landing spot) and start counting from there. Count like this: one, two, three — *one*; one, two, three — *two*; one, two, three — *three,* and so on.

Stop counting when you're about one long step from the base of the second fence (the take-off point). What number did you get? Four? If your horse has an average stride and he doesn't have to work really hard to get to his fences, then you can aim for four. But if you are riding a pony or a stocky, short-legged horse, his natural stride is going to be shorter, so you would most likely ride the line in five.

Knowing how to count strides comes in handy when you go to shows and walk the courses before your classes. You should practice walking and counting strides between fences with a trainer or an experienced horse person. It can take a while to get the hang of counting strides, but don't worry; you'll figure it out!

Do the Math

Average horse stride = 12 feet. (Average pony stride = 10 feet.)
Add a stride for take-off and landing.

STRIDES BETWEEN FENCES	CALCULATION	TOTAL DISTANCE BETWEEN JUMPS
3	(3 × 12) + 12	48 feet
4	(4 × 12) + 12	60 feet
5	(5 × 12) + 12	72 feet

Cantering a Course

Set up a simple course with 7 or 8 jumps in the figure-eight pattern you jumped at the trot (see page 28). Before you begin the course, think through what lead you should be on when you approach the first fence. Trot in a circle (sometimes called a courtesy circle) near the "in-gate" and then pick up the lead you want to be on. Canter the circle one more time to establish a nice rhythm — not too fast, not too slow.

You won't stay on this lead all the way around the course, because courses contain changes of direction. You may jump a fence on the right lead and then have to slow down to a trot and pick up the left lead to head to the next fence. It's not a great idea to approach a fence on the wrong lead, because your horse will become unbalanced and may jump it badly.

If you're riding an experienced horse, you can ask for a flying lead change in the air over the fence or a stride or two after you land. A flying lead change is when your horse changes leads while cantering.

Some horses naturally do flying lead changes to balance themselves, but most need to be taught how to do them. We'll show you how to ask for a flying change and how to teach your horse to do one in the next chapter. (See page 40.) Until you and your horse master flying changes, it's easiest to slow him down to the trot for a stride or two after landing and then ask for the new lead.

Setting up a Double

Why don't you set up a double in your arena? The jumps should be about 24 feet apart for one stride and 36 for two strides.

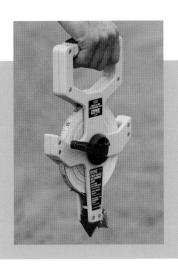

Buy or Borrow a Tape Measure

A regular tape measure from a hardware store isn't long enough to measure out jumping distances, so you might invest in a special longer one (usually a minimum of 100 feet long) just for show jumping. Look for them at tack shops or in equine supply catalogs. If you have a trainer, she or he might let you borrow one to set up some lines.

Seeing Double

As you become more experienced, you'll jump trickier courses. Most advanced courses contain combination fences. A combination is a series of two (a double) or three fences (a triple) that are placed one after the other, with a set distance between them that allows for only one or two canter strides. The first fence in a double is usually a spread and the second fence is an upright.

Before you jump a double, walk it to figure out how many strides your horse will take between fences. If you're at a show, watch other riders canter through a double. Count their strides to figure out how many you would take at the same fence.

You can trot or canter into a double. As you approach the first fence, look straight ahead at the second fence and get into jumping position. On landing, sit back down in the saddle gently. Squeeze your horse's sides to keep him moving forward in an active, bouncy canter. Follow your horse's head with your hands so you don't jab him in the mouth. Count the strides if it helps you to keep the same rhythm between the fences. If the fences are the correct distance apart, your horse should be able to figure out the striding himself.

As you approach the second fence, look over it rather than at it. Then get into jumping position again

Keep looking straight ahead as you jump a double.

and pop over the fence. It's important to jump the first fence of a double nicely, because if you jump awkwardly over the first fence, it's hard to keep a good pace between the two jumps and you might have a bad second fence, too.

Practice, Practice, Practice!

As with anything else, practice makes perfect in jumping. If it's possible, try to work over fences at least once a week so your jumping skills will develop and improve. But don't jump the same fence a hundred times, because your horse will get bored and too much jumping can be stressful on his joints.

In the next chapter you'll learn some exercises that will make learning how to jump even more fun and interesting for you and your horse.

Becoming a good jumper takes lots of practice.

CHAPTER 3
Jumping Exercises

GRID:
A straight line of carefully spaced fences.

TROTTING POLE:
A pole or series of poles placed on the ground to teach a horse to go over an obstacle.

PLACING POLE:
A pole placed 9 feet in front of a jump to help the horse take off at the right spot.

NOT EVERYONE HAS ACCESS to an arena and 10 fences. Most of us make do with a couple of rickety jumps and some hay bales! But a lack of fences doesn't mean you can't practice jumping. All you need are four jumps and a few poles to set up some helpful exercises. And if you're lucky enough to have lots of jumps, you can set up a course.

If you have a few jumps set up in your arena or field, you can pop over them whenever you feel like it, so jumping becomes part of your riding routine. Jumping your horse regularly will help to keep him calm when he jumps during a lesson or at a show. You don't have to jump him every day though. This can put too much stress and strain on his delicate legs. Just once or twice a week should be enough for an experienced horse.

Beginning with Poles

To start training your horse over poles, place several poles randomly around your arena and incorporate them into your flat work sessions. If you're trotting a circle, trot over a pole. Don't get in jumping position; just keep rising to the trot. Ask your horse to walk, trot, or canter over the pole in stride. If he jumps over it, slow him down and stick to the same pole until he simply steps over it.

Pole Courses

Trotting over poles is good practice for both you and your horse, but try different patterns to keep it interesting.

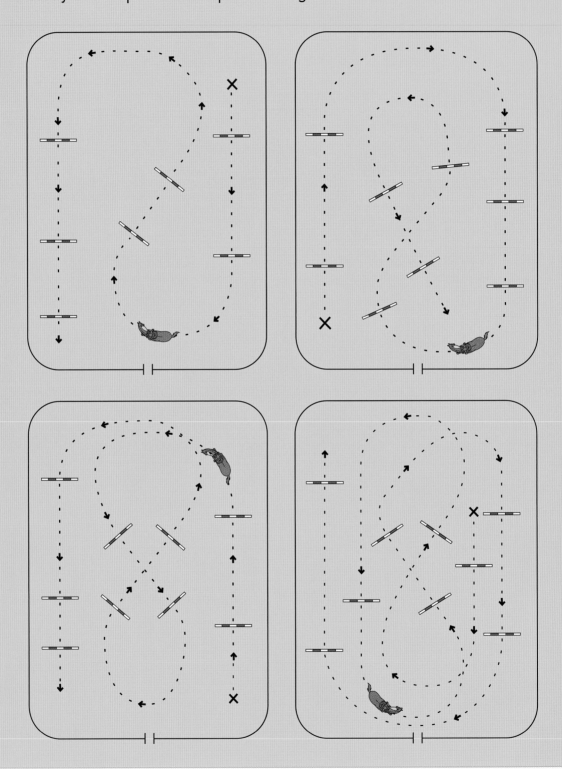

Once your horse is trotting and cantering comfortably over individual poles, set up a course of poles around the arena and trot and canter over it. Concentrate on riding over the middle of the poles and keeping your horse at a consistent pace. Don't let him speed up or slow down in front of a pole. Try this both at a rising trot and in jumping position.

Another exercise is to put a pole on the ground on the track of a 20-meter circle. Trot and canter around the 20-meter circle, stepping over the pole as you go round. Try to keep your horse's pace steady — he might try to speed up when he spots the pole.

When your horse can canter calmly over one pole, add another pole on the other side of the circle. Then add two more so there are four poles in total.

If your horse is well balanced, make the circle smaller. See if he can manage a 15-meter circle, but don't go any smaller because working in tiny circles can be physically difficult for your horse, especially if he isn't very supple. Going round and round in small circles puts a lot of strain on the joints and muscles in your horse's legs.

Place four poles on a 20-meter circle and as you work in the ring, trot and canter over them.

Flying Lead Changes over a Pole

When you're jumping at a show, you need to be on the correct lead all the way around the course. Because you have to change directions on a course, you have to change your horse's leads, too. If he canters round on the wrong lead, he'll be unbalanced and may jump badly, and you'll lose points with the judge.

Very experienced horses can change their leads in the air over a fence so that they land on the correct lead. Others change after they land. You'll do better in shows if your horse changes his leading leg over the fence. Here's how you can teach him to do that.

Start by doing simple lead changes on a figure eight. A simple change is when you slow the canter to a trot before asking for the opposite lead. Pick up the canter to the right and do two loops of canter on the right lead. When you come to the straight line in the middle of the "8" the second time, slow down to a trot for four or five strides and then ask your horse to pick up the left lead and do two loops of canter.

The next time you get back to the middle, take fewer trot strides. Can you pick up the other lead in three strides? Two strides? One stride? Try it! Only spend about five minutes doing this exercise, because it can be boring for your horse.

When your horse has mastered the simple change exercise, set up one pole in the center of the arena as the middle of a figure eight. Trot over the pole a few times while completing the figure eight. Then pick up the canter to the right. As you canter over the pole, give your horse the cues for picking up the left lead: turn his head slightly to the left, press with your inside leg, and give him a kick with your outside leg behind the girth.

If he changes his lead, do a few circles on the left lead and then head back to the pole. As you cross the pole, give him the cues for picking up the right lead: turn his head slightly to the right, press with your inside leg, and give him a kick with your outside leg behind the girth.

Your horse may not pick this up right away, but with practice he will learn how to do a flying change. If you're having real problems switching leads in the air, sign up for a few flat work lessons with a good trainer.

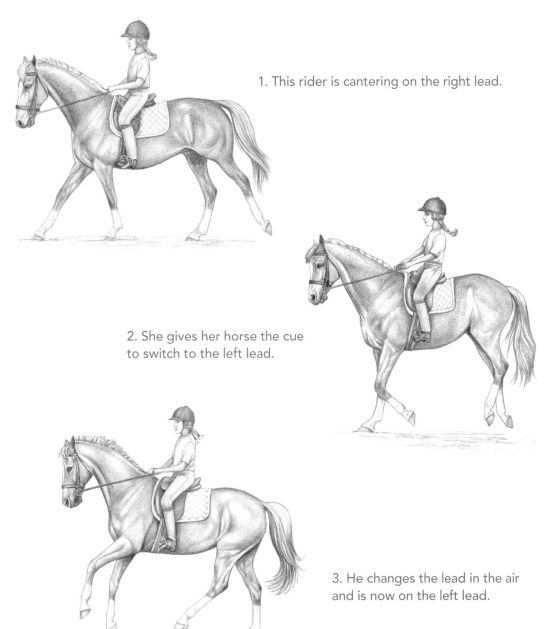

1. This rider is cantering on the right lead.

2. She gives her horse the cue to switch to the left lead.

3. He changes the lead in the air and is now on the left lead.

Fun with Four Fences

If you have only a few fences, you can still improve your jumping skills. Here are three exercises that can be set up easily with four fences. Set the fences up as cross-rails or as verticals with ground poles on both sides so that you can jump all of them from either direction.

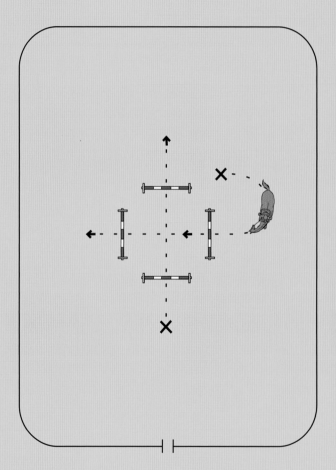

EXERCISE 1

Set up the four fences in a square with one stride (approximately 24 feet) or two strides (approximately 36 feet) between them. You can jump these "doubles" from any direction and pretend you're jumping a course.

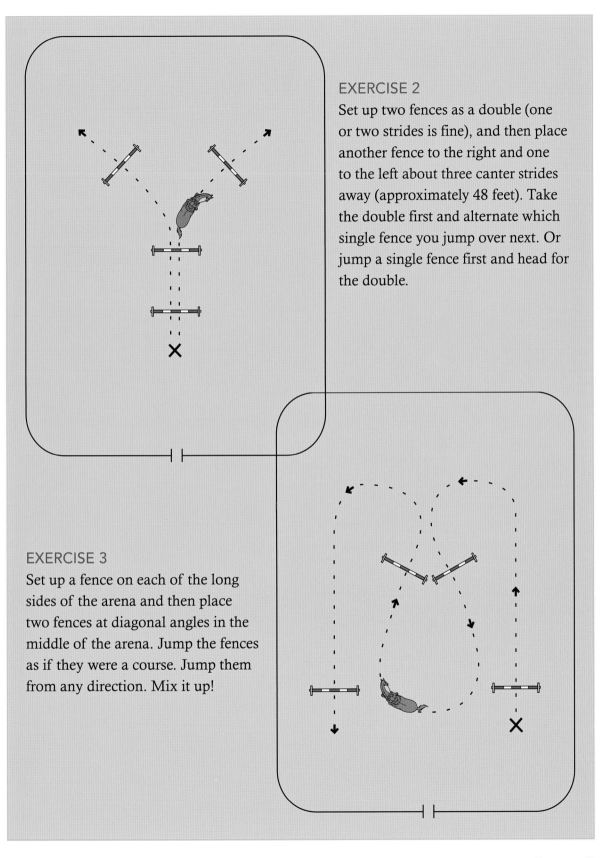

EXERCISE 2

Set up two fences as a double (one or two strides is fine), and then place another fence to the right and one to the left about three canter strides away (approximately 48 feet). Take the double first and alternate which single fence you jump over next. Or jump a single fence first and head for the double.

EXERCISE 3

Set up a fence on each of the long sides of the arena and then place two fences at diagonal angles in the middle of the arena. Jump the fences as if they were a course. Jump them from any direction. Mix it up!

Grids

A grid is a straight line of carefully spaced fences and poles that you jump with your horse. If a grid is set up properly, with the correct spacing between jumps, your horse should jump it easily. Grid work is sometimes called gymnastics. Here are some of the benefits of grids:

- Grids build up your horse's confidence. If he's a spooky jumper or refuses a lot, grids can improve his jumping.
- Grids make your horse more flexible.
- Grids boost your confidence, too. Because most horses find them easy, you can concentrate on your riding position.

Grid Layout

The top distances are for a horse, the bottom ones for a pony.

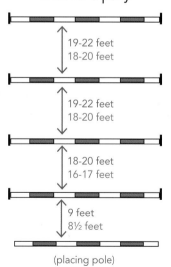

19-22 feet
18-20 feet

19-22 feet
18-20 feet

18-20 feet
16-17 feet

9 feet
8½ feet

(placing pole)

Start with trotting poles, then set up cross-rails, then verticals as you gain experience.

Setting Up a Grid

The most important thing you need when jumping a grid is a helper! A person on the ground can adjust the distances between the fences if your horse is having trouble jumping the grid. Your helper can also be your eyes on the ground. She'll be able to tell you if you need to use more leg to ask your horse to speed up or let you know if you need to slow your horse down so he's more careful over the jumps. And she can shout out helpful hints like "Look forward — not down!"

Set up a simple grid with four cross-rail fences. Put a "placing pole" about 9 feet (3 human strides) in front of the first fence. A placing pole helps your horse take off at the correct spot. Set up the fences one stride apart. This means that your horse lands after one fence, takes one stride, and then takes off again over the next fence.

It's important to set distances that are correct for your horse. If your horse stumbles or jumps much higher than necessary for a fence, your helper needs to move the fences closer together or farther apart. Don't make your horse jump bad distances, because you'll damage his confidence. Remember that a pony has shorter strides than a horse, so if you're riding a horse and your pal is on a pony, you won't be able to jump the same grid.

A grid must be measured accurately so a horse will jump it easily.

Distances

The first two fences should be slightly closer together because you're trotting in to the first fence and your horse will land closer to the fence than he would if he was cantering.

When he canters into a fence he lands farther away from the fence, so the distance between those two fences needs to be slightly wider.

Let's Go

To start working on a grid, set up a series of trotting poles on the ground between pairs of standards. Warm up your horse on the flat, then pick up an active, bouncy trot and head for the grid. Get into jumping position before you arrive at the placing pole and remain in it throughout the grid.

Keep your legs on your horse, soften your hold on the reins, and aim for the middle of the poles. Maintain the same trot throughout the grid. If your horse trips or knocks a pole, he may be going too slowly, or the poles might not be the perfect distance apart for him and need to be adjusted.

After you've been through the grid a few times, ask your helper to put up a small cross-rail fence at the end. Your horse might want to canter over the cross-rail. It's okay to trot into the grid and canter out. Sit quietly and

Your first grid should be made up of only trotting poles.

Next, set up a small cross-rail fence at the end of the trotting poles.

let him figure out the grid for himself. Keep your legs on his sides to encourage him to move forward.

When you are comfortable with this configuration, ask your helper to put up a cross-rail fence at the beginning of the grid, so that your horse jumps into the grid, canters over two poles, and then jumps the last fence. If he jumps the grid nicely a couple of times, you can add more cross-rails, until he's jumping a whole row of cross-rails.

Finish up by making the last fence a small vertical. After you've jumped the grid smoothly, make the second to last fence a vertical, too.

(LEFT) Put several tiny cross-rail fences in the grid to make it more challenging. (RIGHT) Make the last fence of the grid a vertical.

Moving On

Learning to jump isn't going to be smooth sailing all the way. Expect some setbacks and frustrations, but don't be too hard on yourself. Remember that you can learn a lot from your mistakes as well as your successes. In the next chapter we'll look at some common problems you may encounter while learning to jump and what you can do about them.

Loosen Up!

Sometimes you need to loosen up and have fun while jumping! Set up a few tiny fences in an arena and try these exercises, always in the jumping position.

▲ Eyes Up! If you have a habit of looking down when you jump, ask a pal to stand in the distance on the far side of a jump. As you head for the jump, she should hold up some fingers on one hand (it doesn't matter how many). Keep an eye on her hand and shout out the number of fingers as you jump.

▲ Bareback! If you are used to riding bareback, and your horse is well behaved and an experienced jumper, you can take off the saddle and jump. Grab hold of some mane to help you stay in jumping position.

▲ One Hand! Keep one hand on the reins and put the other one on your hip when you jump.

▲ No Spill! Hold the reins in one hand and hold a plastic mug half-filled with water in the other hand. See if you can jump the fence without spilling any water. Watch out — you might get wet!

◄ No Hands! If you're feeling brave, knot your reins and pop over a tiny fence with your arms outstretched. This will really test your balance! Push those heels down to keep you secure in the saddle.

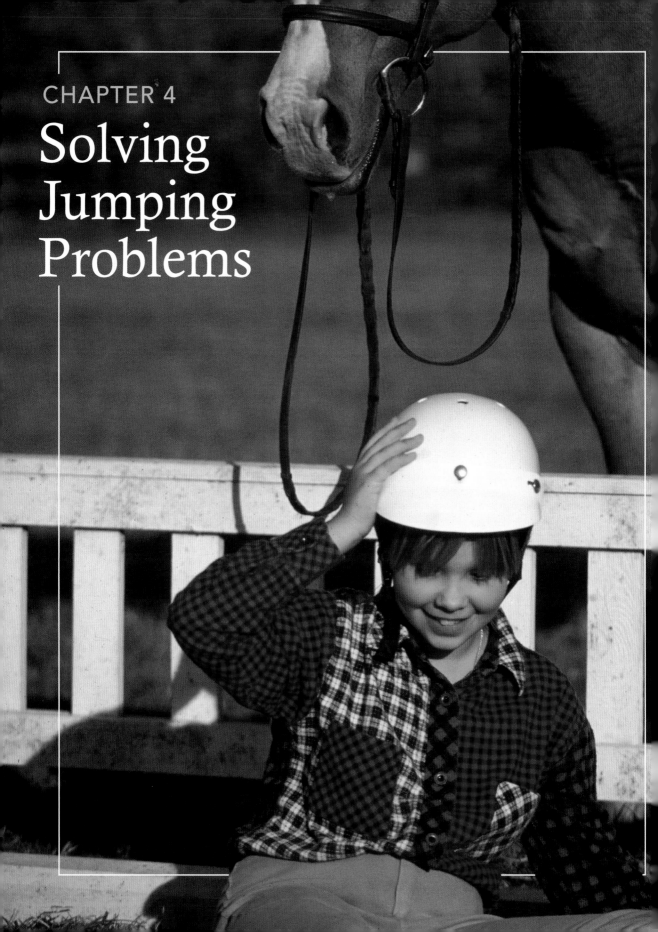

CHAPTER 4

Solving Jumping Problems

Horse Talk

DUCKING:
When a rider leans to one side while jumping over a fence.

REFUSAL
(also stopping or quitting):
When a horse refuses to jump a fence.

RUN-OUT:
When a horse darts to the right or the left to avoid a jump.

Lots of things can go wrong when you're jumping, which is why it takes a long time to learn to jump well and is also why people fall off! Your horse may slam on the brakes right in front of a fence. He may run out to the side or knock down a pole. Here are a few reasons why jumping problems are so common.

Inexperience. Your horse simply doesn't know how to jump or hasn't been taught to jump properly. If you're new to jumping, you might be causing the problems. You might be pulling him on the mouth and confusing him. Or you could be bouncing around in the saddle and making him unbalanced.

Lack of confidence. If your horse is being asked to jump fences that are too big, he may get nervous and refuse to jump. And if you're trying to jump a fence that you think is scary, you might not feel confident. Horses are sensitive creatures so if you're feeling nervous, your horse will, too!

Poorly fitting tack. A saddle that pinches his withers or constricts the movement of his shoulder can make jumping unpleasant for your horse. A poorly fitted bridle could pinch him, and a bit that is too low in his mouth could bang him in the teeth. Make sure that your horse's tack is comfortable and correctly fitted. If it's not, you'll continue to have problems.

Badly spaced fences. If your horse has trouble jumping a line or a double every single time, it may be because the fences are badly spaced and he can't get the correct striding. Grab a jumping tape measure and check that the distances between jumps are suitable for the size of your horse.

Health problems. A horse might refuse to jump if he's in pain. He might have arthritis in his leg joints that makes it difficult for him to jump. Or his back might hurt. He might have a foot problem that requires special shoeing.

Ring sourness. Your horse may be bored with jumping. Have you been working him more than a few times a week? Have you been working only on jumping and nothing else? Every horse needs a break from the ring and from work! Get him out of the arena and canter around a big field. Go on a fun trail ride with a friend. Ride and relax!

If your horse isn't jumping well, he might have a physical problem. Ask your vet to give him a checkup.

Making a Difficult Decision

Be realistic about your horse's ability and interest in jumping. Some horses will never be comfortable jumping more than a certain height, so accept your horse's limitations. If you have problems every time you jump him and he just doesn't improve — even after regular lessons with a trainer — it might be time to think about giving your horse another job.

If you want to jump higher and higher and to compete in shows, and your horse isn't going to make the grade, you might have to think about buying another horse.

Sometimes a physical problem is causing your horse to balk at jumping. If you suspect that your horse isn't feeling 100 percent, have your veterinarian give him a thorough checkup. The veterinarian may recommend massage therapy or chiropractic care to make your horse feel better.

If your horse is older and has arthritis, his hocks and ankles may need to be injected with a lubricating substance to make jumping easier for him. If your horse is fairly old, say 25 or older, he may not be physically able to leap over a fence anymore, and he may need to be retired from jumping. You can still have fun with him by doing easy flat work in the arena and going out on relaxing trail rides.

You need to talk seriously with your parents and your trainer. If you really love your horse, it will be difficult to let him go. But if you find him a great home where he's doing something he enjoys, like trail riding, you won't miss him quite as much and you can begin your search for a more suitable jumping partner.

If you live on a farm or your parents will allow you to have two horses, maybe you can keep your old horse as a companion to your new horse. Or perhaps you can find a younger, less experienced child to lease him and love him as much as you do.

Common Jumping Problems

Jumping is lots of fun, but it takes time and practice to learn to do it well. There are plenty of things that can go wrong as you are learning. Here are some of the problems that you might encounter.

Refusals

A "refusal" is when your horse stops right in front of a fence. Refusals are frustrating, especially if they cause you to fall off and eat dirt! They also can contribute to losing your confidence. But remember that even the best riders in the world sometimes fall when a horse stops suddenly or veers off course.

If your horse begins to refuse quite often, you need to figure out why before the problem gets worse. If you don't already take regular lessons, sign up with a trainer who can help you and your horse get back on track. The trainer might notice that your horse ignores your leg aids. For example, if he doesn't respond to a squeeze or kick, he won't have enough impulsion to jump a fence nicely.

Stopping in front of a fence is called a "refusal."

It's easy for a horse to stop if he's just moseying along in front of a fence. If this is the case, go back to working on the flat for a while to sharpen up your horse's reactions to your leg aids. If he doesn't move forward when you squeeze with your legs, give him a kick. If he still doesn't respond, tap him with a crop behind your lower leg. Wake him up!

You may be asking your horse to jump a fence that he's not yet ready to jump. Always start small when jumping and move up to bigger fences gradually. If your horse refuses 3-foot fences, go back to 2-foot fences for a while. When he jumps smaller fences nicely, raise the poles 6 inches.

Grids can help boost your horse's confidence about jumping.

Don't jump him over a course of 3-foot fences right away. Mix bigger fences in with smaller fences, and do some grid work. Grids are great confidence boosters for you and your horse.

When your horse refuses, don't make a big deal out of it. If the fence is small, back him up a step or two and then kick him on with your calves and tap him with the crop so he moves forward quickly and jumps the fence. If the fence is larger than 2 feet 6 inches, trot or canter him in a small circle, don't give him a lot of time to think about the refusal, and aim him at the jump again. Ride strongly and bravely to encourage him to jump.

One of the top causes of refusals is the rider's poor jumping position. You may be leaning too far forward over your horse's neck and unbalancing him. You could be throwing your hands up in the air and trying to lift him over the fence. Work on perfecting your jumping position on the flat before you pop over any more fences.

A "run-out" is when a horse avoids jumping by darting to the right or the left of the fence.

Run-outs

A "run-out" is when a horse goes to the right or the left and runs away from the jump. Most run-outs are the result of not steering a horse into a fence properly. He may also run out because you are unbalanced in the saddle. If you're leaning to the left, he may use that as an excuse to run out to the left. He may also take the opportunity to avoid the fence if your reins are too loose.

If your horse runs out, turn right around in a small half circle and immediately approach the fence again. Don't make a big circle and give your horse a long approach to the fence. Remember, most horses and ponies can jump 3 feet from a standstill. To avoid run-outs, keep a fairly strong hold on the reins and make sure both reins are even. Put your leg strongly on your horse about 4 feet away from the fence and steer him or her to the middle of the poles.

You may notice that your horse tends to run out on one side more than another. If he runs out to the left, press the left rein into his neck and move your right rein slightly out to the side. Hold a crop in your left hand and press it on his shoulder. Your left leg should be at the girth and applying lots of pressure to prevent him from darting out.

If your horse runs out to the right, use the opposite aids: right hand and rein on the neck, left rein and hand out to the side. Carry the crop in your right hand and use your right leg more strongly than your left.

If your horse runs out a lot, your helper on the ground can place two poles so they rest on the jump and form "wings" out to the sides. These poles should help keep your horse aiming at the middle of the fence. If he jumps the fence nicely a few times, you can place these poles on the ground.

Of course, your horse may run out because the jumps are too high. Restore his confidence by going back to smaller jumps and work up again slowly.

Setting poles up in a V-shape helps to prevent run-outs.

Solving Jumping Problems **57**

Knocking Down Poles

Your horse may knock down poles because he's inexperienced or because he's being lazy. Or you may be sending unclear or mixed signals. Always look to your own riding first if you are having problems.

One way to help him jump more cleanly is to place a saddle pad or blanket over a small vertical and jump him over it. He should look at the "filler" and pick up his feet to clear it. A placing pole situated 9 feet in front of the fence will help him take off in the right place and clear the fence in style.

Rushing

Rushing is when a horse approaches a fence too fast. A horse who rushes is likely to take off too far back, and there's a good chance he's going to knock down poles.

If your horse rushes, ask him to halt about 10 feet away from the fence and then walk up to it before jumping.

Placing poles in front of and after the fence will slow down your horse.

If you ride a rusher, go back to flat work. Make sure you can control him at the canter and adjust his speed over poles on the ground before you jump again.

If your horse begins to rush while you are schooling over fences, circle a few times and slow him down before approaching again. Ask him to halt and then walk from about 10 feet away from a small fence. Let him jump it from the walk, and pick up the trot again after you land.

You can also try setting a placing pole 9 feet in front of the fence and 9 feet after the fence. These poles will encourage him to slow down before and after the fence.

Another option is to try the following arena exercises to help you slow down your horse at the canter and make him listen to you more.

EXERCISE 1

Set up three poles on the ground about 9 feet apart (three big human strides) and canter over them. The distances are a bit tight so your horse will have to shorten his stride to canter over them without breaking stride or knocking a pole. Really concentrate on keeping his canter bouncy — don't let him get strung out and gallop over the poles.

Canter over three poles set about 9 feet apart.

EXERCISE 2

1. Pick up the canter and head around the arena. When you get to the short end of the arena, ask your horse to slow down and canter a 20-meter circle in a nice, bouncy, collected canter.
2. Circle twice and then head out to the long side of the arena.
3. Loosen your hold on the reins and ask your horse with your legs to canter forward strongly. You want him almost at a gallop, but not quite. He should listen to your legs and move forward at a brisk pace.
4. When you reach the short side of the arena, take up your contact again on the reins, slow him down, and put him back on a 20-meter circle. Once again he should canter with impulsion.
5. After circling twice, loosen the reins and ask him to canter forward down the long side of the arena. Repeat this exercise one more time and then let your horse rest.

Cantering in a circle helps you work on control.

Common Rider Problems

Jumping takes teamwork and sometimes it is the rider who is causing the problems over the jumps. If you ride by yourself a lot, you might be slipping into bad riding habits. Perhaps your heels aren't down far enough or you aren't sitting up straight.

This is why you should try to take regular lessons. Having a trainer watch you from the ground can really make a difference in your position and riding style. She will be able to point out things you might be doing wrong and help you fix them.

If you are having trouble jumping, look at some of these possible explanations.

Ducking

"Ducking" is when a rider leans to one side while jumping over a fence. Ducking can unbalance a horse, which may cause him to knock down a pole or land unevenly. If your trainer says that you're ducking, concentrate on looking forward through your horse's ears and over the fence as you approach and jump it. Keep your upper body over your horse's neck and don't fall to one side.

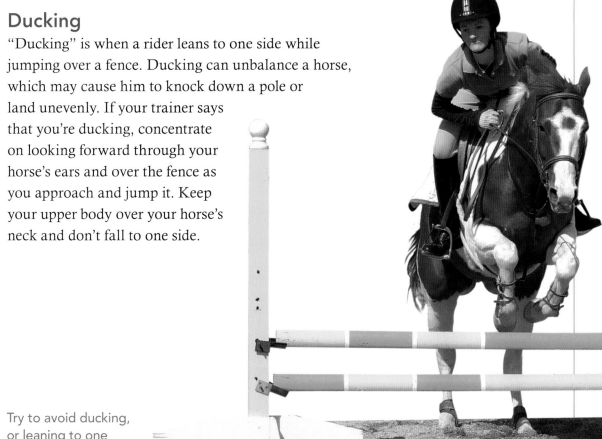

Try to avoid ducking, or leaning to one side, while jumping over a fence.

Getting Left Behind

If you don't stay with your horse's motion when he jumps and you are momentarily thrown backward and a few inches above the saddle, you've been "left behind!" Getting left behind is uncomfortable for you and your horse, because you land back in the saddle with a big bump and are likely to yank on the bit.

Avoid being left behind by getting into jumping position a stride or two away from the fence and grabbing hold of some mane or a neck strap. Push down your heels and keep your legs close to the girth. If your legs shoot forward, you increase your chance of being left behind.

Practice jumping position on the flat and over poles. Once you can stay in jumping position at the canter and hand gallop, you can pop over a fence without falling out of position.

Doing lots of jumping position while you ride on the flat will strengthen your legs and improve your balance.

Leaning and Over-jumping

Leaning too far forward makes your legs slide back and your heels come up. If your horse refuses while you're in this insecure position, you may fly over his head. Try to press your heels down and keep your bottom close to the saddle while you bend at the waist without moving your whole body forward.

Sometimes riders throw themselves over a fence before their horse even has a chance to leave the ground. Other riders raise their hands to try to lift their horses over the fence. These sloppy riding habits, called over-jumping, can unbalance a horse and make him jump badly.

Swinging Legs

If your lower legs swing back and forth while you jump, your stirrups are too long. Shorten them a hole or two to make it easier to keep your legs in place. Short stirrups are like seatbelts in a car. They keep you safe and secure in the saddle. You should also practice your jumping position at the walk, trot, and canter. Jumping position strengthens your legs and the stronger your legs are, the steadier they will be.

Shorter stirrups keep your legs from swinging and make your position steadier.

A good trainer will set up jumping exercises that build your confidence.

Rider Nerves

Even though jumping can be tons of fun, it can sometimes be scary and you might feel nervous. Your horse is a sensitive animal, and he can tell when you are scared because it shows up in your riding position and your cues. If you feel nervous about jumping a fence, your horse will feel nervous, too.

If you feel really scared about jumping, go back to small fences until you build your confidence back up. If you have a trainer, be honest with her about your feelings. If she's a good trainer, she won't force you to jump anything that scares you. A good trainer makes jumping fun. If you feel calm and confident, your horse is more likely to jump the fences in front of him.

Falling Off

It can be scary when you fall off while jumping, but if you aren't injured, it is best to catch your horse and remount. Work him for a few minutes on the flat so you can regain your composure and your concentration, and try to jump the problem fence again. There's nothing wrong with lowering the fence before you try it again.

The more opportunities you have to jump at home or at the barn, the more confident both you and your horse will become — and the fewer chances there will be for refusals and run-outs. So it's important that you have at least a couple of jumps to practice with.

In the next chapter, we show you how to create inexpensive jumps of your own and design basic courses for you and your horse to leap over!

Falling off isn't the end of the world. Just hop back on and continue riding.

Helmet Safety

If you fall off while riding on the flat or jumping and hit your head hard on a fence or the ground, it's a good idea to replace your helmet. Why? Your helmet may have cracked or become weaker in places and it may not protect you properly if you fall off again.

Some helmet manufacturers will replace the helmet at a discounted price. Go to your helmet manufacturer's Web site to see what its policy is on replacing damaged helmets.

CHAPTER 5

Building Jumps and Designing Courses

IF YOU KEEP YOUR HORSE at home or at a small barn, you may not have fences to jump. Don't worry, you can make your own. Building jumps doesn't cost a ton of money and it's not difficult. If one of your parents is handy with a hammer, saw, and drill, you can whip up simple fences in no time at all.

If you board at a barn without any jumps, check with the barn owner to make sure she doesn't mind if you build some jumps and put them in the arena. She may not want people jumping at her barn, because jumping is a risky activity and she might be required to buy extra insurance. Riders are much more likely to hurt themselves while jumping than while riding on the flat.

Building a Pair of Standards

Standards, also called "wings," are the vertical frames that hold up the poles. You can make a pair of standards using wood from any building supply store. Here's what you'll need to build one pair of standards.

Tool list

A saw

A screwdriver

A drill with a ¼-inch regular bit and ½-inch spade bit

Material list

One 8-foot length of treated 4×4 wood

Two 8-foot lengths of treated 1×4 wood

A box of 1½-inch wood screws

One pair of jump cups

Directions

1. Cut the 8-foot section of 4×4 into two 4-foot long pieces. These are the uprights that hold the jump cups.
2. Cut each 8-foot plank into 2-foot sections, for a total of eight pieces. These form the horizontal feet that hold the uprights in place.

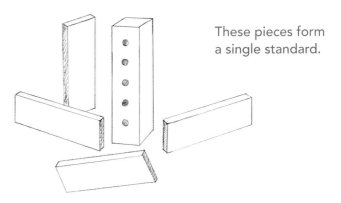

These pieces form a single standard.

3. With the spade bit, drill holes in 3-inch increments along the 4×4 upright. The holes should go all the way through.
4. Set the upright on a table or pair of sawhorses. Using three screws in a triangular pattern, attach one of the 2-foot plank sections flush along the bottom edge of the post as shown.

Three screws are sturdier than two.

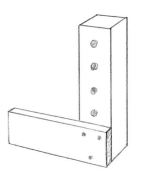

5. Attach each remaining foot at a 90-degree angle to the previous one, forming a pinwheel pattern at the base of the upright.

You can buy metal or plastic jump cups at a tack shop or order them out of a horse catalog or over the Internet. Plastic jump cups are more expensive but they don't rust.

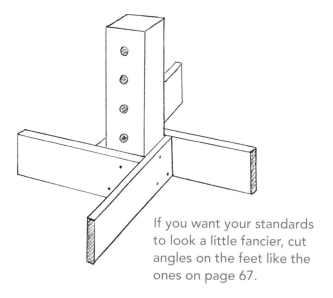

If you want your standards to look a little fancier, cut angles on the feet like the ones on page 67.

Poles

The easiest way to make jump poles is to buy a bunch of the 8-foot wooden poles you find in the gardening section at most building supply stores. These are inexpensive, treated landscaping poles that are used for garden borders. They are rounded at the corners and fit well into jump cups. Painted in stripes with outdoor paint, they make pretty good jump poles.

If your family has a table saw that cuts on an angle, you can buy 10- or 12-foot lengths of 4×4 and ask your mom or dad to cut off the corners to make them more rounded. Paint these poles white and add colorful stripes. You can also buy adhesive jump tape that wraps around the poles to make stripes. This tape comes in several bright colors and is made of waterproof vinyl. Look for it at a tack store or in catalogs.

Some people use plastic plumbing pipes, but they are too light, and they can break and splinter if your horse steps on them or knocks them over.

Bargain Paint

Outdoor paint for your jumps can be expensive, so look for bargains. Sometimes people custom order paint and then they refuse to buy it. The hardware store places it on a discount rack, where it's much cheaper than regular paint. Look and see what colors are on offer, but make sure it's outside paint before you buy.

Straw or hay bales, fir tree branches, and horse blankets all make good fillers.

Fillers

It's a good idea to have fillers in your jumps at home, so your horse gets used to them and is less likely to spook or refuse a solid-looking jump at a show. Here are some items you can use to make a pole jump seem more solid:

- Straw or hay bales
- Fir tree branches
- Buckets turned upside down
- Horse blankets or saddle pads
- Wooden pallets
- Flower "boxes"

To use pallets as fillers, saw them in half and nail or screw wooden feet on them so they don't tip over. Paint them white and fill them with nonpoisonous fir tree branches.

Drill holes in a 4x4 piece of treated wood and put inexpensive plastic flowers in the holes. Very pretty!

Large plastic barrels also make great fillers and you can use them as standards, too. Place poles on top of the barrels to make an upright fence or create a simple cross-pole fence by resting one end of each pole on the ground. Most barrels are about 2 feet high when they're lying on their sides — perfect for popping over! Put two end to end to create a wider jump. You can use a pair of standards to hold them in place.

You can find empty soap barrels at car wash centers for a couple of dollars. Hose out the barrel with water to rinse out leftover soap or chemicals before you use it.

Make a Splash!

Many show jumping courses contain a water jump, sometimes called a "Liverpool." This is usually a shallow pool made out of rubber. It's filled with water and goes under a jump. You can make your own water jump by buying a blue tarpaulin. Fold it in half, lay it on the ground under a jump, and weigh it down with two poles.

If your horse is spooky, train him to walk over the tarp without the jump pole in place before you try jumping it. When you do jump it the first few times, be prepared in case he leaps it *big*. Hang on to some mane so you don't get thrown out of the saddle.

You may have to pop over a water jump on a jumper course or an eventing stadium course.

Make a fake Liverpool with a blue tarp and two poles and walk your horse over it a couple of times before jumping it.

Eventing Fences

Eventing includes three disciplines: dressage, show jumping in an arena, and cross-country with jumps. Arena show jumping fences are designed to fall down if your horse hits them, but cross-country fences are always solid. If you hit them hard, they don't fall down, so it's important to start small and work your way up to bigger jumps.

You should practice jumping solid jumps, but it's not always possible to ride on cross-country courses because many are on private land and open to the public only occasionally. But you can make some practice jumps at home for your arena or your horse's field. It's a good idea to practice jumping some solid-looking fences at home, so that when your horse gets to a horse trial (event) he doesn't faint at the sight of a log pile or a jump made of straw bales.

On the next two pages are some cross-country type fences you can make and practice over at home. You can build a small eventing course by putting these jumps around the edge of a field. Space them widely so that you can have a good canter between jumps.

At big-time events like Rolex Kentucky Three-Day Event, corner jumps are often made from stone walls or solid wood. You must be very accurate and steer your horse straight when jumping a corner fence, or he might run out.

Cross-country Jumps

▲ Tires.
Hang four or five tires over a jump pole between two standards to make a solid-looking eventing-type fence. You can also lean them on their sides against a jumping pole. Small car tires make great beginner fences. If you want to jump bigger fences, use sport utility vehicle or truck tires.

▲ Hay or Straw Bales.
Grab three hay or straw bales and place them in a row end to end. If you want to make the fence bigger, use six bales and stack them two high.

▶ Mock Ditch.
Fold a dark tarp into a rectangle about 8 feet long and 2 feet wide. Place it on the ground and secure it with two poles so it doesn't flap around. As your horse canters toward it, he can't tell it's not a hole.

It might be a good idea to place jump standards on either side of the mock ditch to help your horse see where it is. Once he becomes more experienced, you can take them away. When you're competing, you probably won't have jump standards defining a ditch, so your horse must learn to jump without them.

► Corner Fence.
A corner fence looks like a V. Set up two standards about 2 feet apart as shown and place a barrel or bale of hay about 8 feet away.

Place one end of a pole in each jump cup and the other end on the barrel or hay bale. Jump a corner fence straight across the V, not at the diagonal.

▲ Skinnies.
A skinny is a narrow fence. You probably won't see one in lower-level eventing, but they're fun to jump and are good practice for you and your horse. Make a skinny out of one barrel. Turn it on its side and put small jump standards on either side of it or rest two poles on the barrel in a V-shape to guide your horse over it.

▲ Log Piles and Single Logs.
If you don't have a tree trunk handy, ask your parents if you can raid the log pile and stack some logs up into a great fence. Make the pile as big or little as you want. Decorate the fence with fir tree branches or pumpkins to make it look more interesting.

It's fun to design and set up a jumping course at home if you have the room.

Designing a Course

Before you head to a show, you need to jump a few courses. This means taking 9 or 10 fences in one go so that your horse learns he must keep moving until you slow him down and not stop after 1 or 2 fences! Think about changing direction at least once.

Start with an inviting cross-rail or small vertical fence so your horse doesn't have a reason to refuse or run out. Then mix in some spreads, and even a water jump if you feel brave! Include a double combination in your course, because your horse may have to jump one at a show.

It's a great idea to practice jumping entire show jumping or cross-country courses, not just one or two fences, on a regular basis so your horse will be prepared for a show jumping course of 8 or 9 fences or a cross-country course of 20 or more fences when you go to a show or event. In the next chapter, we'll talk about what other things you and your horse can expect at a competition.

Simple Course Designs

KEY: ┣━━━┫ vertical ▦▦▦ spread ▨▨▨ wall ✗ = start

CHAPTER 6

Jumping at a Show

COURTESY CIRCLE:
A small circle trotted or cantered at the beginning of a competitor's trip around a jump course.

FAULTS:
Penalty points assessed in competition for mistakes such as knocking down a rail or picking up the wrong lead.

Going to a show is a great way to see how well you've trained your horse or pony to jump, and let's face it, it feels really great to come home with a ribbon or two! But jumping at a show is a lot different than jumping at home because there's so much going on: horses getting on and off trailers, ponies trotting around, people practicing in the warm-up arena, a noisy crowd, loud announcers, and colorful fences your pony has never seen (or jumped) before. All of this can be overwhelming for a young or inexperienced horse or a rider at her first show.

To make your first showing experience a positive one, you need to do a few things before loading your horse on the trailer and heading for the show grounds. Set yourself up for success! To start, you must be capable of walking, trotting, and cantering with confidence, and of jumping your horse without any problems. It is important that you are able to stop him immediately.

You must also feel confident that your horse is well behaved and will not buck, rear, or run off with you. If he bucks or rears at home, he'll probably do it at a show. This kind of behavior is always dangerous, but especially in a situation where there are lots of horses and riders who could get hurt if your horse acts up.

One way to prepare your horse is to make sure he is used to riding with other

horses. Sign up for a few group lessons or go on a trail ride with several friends. Your horse needs to be comfortable around lots of other horses before you try to school him in a crowded warm-up arena. Ask some of your friends to meet you in the arena and have them trot and canter behind your horse. Line up like you would in a show and ask your horses to stand patiently for a moment or two.

If you plan to jump at the show, make sure that you have jumped fences as high, or higher, than the ones at the show. If you want to enter a 2-foot jumping class, you should be jumping 2 feet 3 inches at home. And put in plenty of time practicing loading your horse on the trailer. Take your time and train him properly so that loading up is just a part of the day, not a big fight. It's very frustrating when your horse won't get on the trailer on the morning of a show!

Some Common Show Terms

Chipping. When your horse adds an extra, tiny step in a line and makes an awkward jump.

Clean round. A jumping round where you have no refusals or run-outs and finish within the time limit.

Division. A collection of related classes at a show.

Faults. Penalties for errors.

Jumping flat. When your horse stretches out his neck and keeps his back flat when jumping.

Limit classes. Open to riders who have won fewer than six blue ribbons.

Loose or dangling front legs. When your horse's front legs flop around over a jump, instead of being nicely tucked up.

Maiden classes. Open to riders who have never won a ribbon.

On deck. The next rider waiting to go in the arena is on deck.

Open classes. Open to all riders no matter how many ribbons they've won.

Rubbed a fence. When your horse touches a fence with his tummy or back legs.

Trip. Your ride around and over a jumping course.

Which Classes to Enter?

If you think you're ready to jump at a show, start by going to a few shows and just watching the various classes. Collect the show programs and decide which jumping classes you feel ready to enter.

There are jumping classes for every level of rider and horse, and most programs will tell you how high you'll have to jump in each class. Pick classes with fence heights you're used to jumping, or even a little lower, to start with.

You must also decide how many classes you're going to enter. If it's your first show, don't enter 10 jumping classes! This is too much work for both you and your horse. Think about entering three jumping classes in one day. This gives you plenty of time to warm up and to relax between classes. Remember, you might want to enter a few flat classes as well, and you don't want to wear out your horse.

Cross-rail and Trotting Pole Classes

Trotting pole and cross-rail classes are for beginner riders or green (inexperienced) horses. Most courses have four poles or fences, two on each long side of the arena. Cross-rail jumps are usually no more than 1½ feet high. Usually you must trot or canter, sticking to the same gait around the whole course. You are judged on how smoothly you jump the course.

Beginner Horse or Rider Classes

These classes are for riders who can jump higher than cross-rails but aren't quite ready to move up to bigger fences. If either you or your horse has already won a blue ribbon in a jumping class, you may not be able to enter this class. The simple course is made up of approximately 10 small verticals and cross-poles. The person who jumps the most accurately and smoothly around the course usually wins.

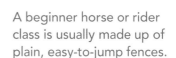

A beginner horse or rider class is usually made up of plain, easy-to-jump fences.

Short-stirrup Classes

If you are aged 12 or younger, you can enter short-stirrup classes. The fences are around 2 feet or 2 feet 3 inches high, and the course is made up of verticals, small walls, and spreads. You might even have to jump a roll top, which is a rounded fence usually covered in artificial grass.

The judge will be looking for a smooth round in which your horse takes off at the right point in front of the fence. She'll expect you to be on the correct lead at all times. If you land on the wrong lead, you must change leads quickly! She'll also be looking at your riding style — how do you look in the saddle?

Hunter Classes

In a hunter class, your horse is judged as you jump the course. The judge wants to see if your horse is obedient and well mannered. If he zips around the course with his head in the air, you won't get high marks. He needs to jump around the course steadily, and you must keep a light contact on his mouth.

Hunter courses are fairly simple and usually have 9 or 10 fences. The fences are made of natural colors like brown, beige, and white. There may be brush fences made out of evergreen branches, and you may have to jump a small wooden gate.

Equitation Classes

In this class, the judge looks at you, not your horse, as you jump the course. She wants to see quiet hands, a secure seat, and strong legs. If you're yanking on your horse's mouth, you won't win this class. It's important that your horse take off at the correct point in front of a fence (about a stride away) and that you jump with him and don't get left behind. The jumps on an equitation course are similar to those in a hunter course.

The judge critiques your jumping style — not your horse's — in an equitation class.

Jumper Classes

Jumper courses usually have 9 or 10 fences. The fences are colorful and may have patterns on them. There will be walls, panels, and roll tops. The course may be tricky, with double and triple fences, tough turns, and twisty paths.

In a jumper class, the only thing that counts is jumping a clear round in the time allowed. If you make it around without knocking down a pole or having a refusal, you'll compete in a timed jump-off against other people who have also gone clear, even if your riding style was a bit messy. The most important thing in the jump-off is speed.

People can cut corners and jump fences at angles to save time, but they also want to jump clear. The fastest round with the least faults wins.

You don't have to do a courtesy circle in a jumper class. Most people just pick up the canter after they hear the bell and head for the first fence.

Jumper courses are made up of colorful fences.

Schooling and Warm-up Classes

Schooling and warm-up classes are held at the beginning of the show — usually early in the morning. It's a good idea to arrive early so you can enter some of these classes, because they give you and your horse the chance to practice over some of the fences you'll jump later in the day. The fences will be small, usually 18 inches or 2 feet. If you've never jumped a wall at a show, a schooling or warm-up class is a great place to do that for the first time.

If you're new to jumping or your horse is green, consider going to a show and just competing in a schooling class or two and then going home. Entering schooling classes is a super way to introduce your horse to jumping at a show because they tend to be more relaxed and you won't get stressed out!

Proper Show Attire

It's a good idea to go to a few shows to check out what people are wearing when they compete. Then you can see if you have the correct items of clothing before you head out to a show.

▶ A typical show outfit for most jumping classes includes a black safety helmet with a fixed chin-strap, a collarless show shirt with a matching choker, dark gloves, light-colored breeches or jodhpurs, a dark (navy, gray, green, or brown is best) coat with sleeves long enough to cover your wrists, and field boots with the laces at the top of the foot.

◀ In jumper classes, just about anything goes. Your horse can wear a running martingale and boots, and you can choose from a variety of nosebands and bits.

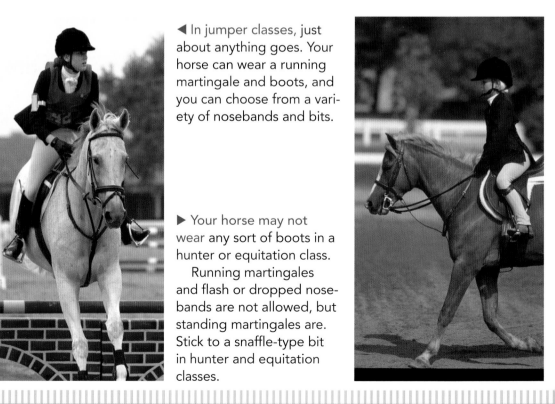

▶ Your horse may not wear any sort of boots in a hunter or equitation class. Running martingales and flash or dropped nose-bands are not allowed, but standing martingales are. Stick to a snaffle-type bit in hunter and equitation classes.

▲ You don't have to wear a jacket in a jumper class. Riders often wear solid-colored polo shirts. Jumper riders often sport sleek, low-profile helmets. Many young riders decorate a stripe on the front of their helmets with rhinestones or ribbon to add some pizzazz to their show outfits!

▲ In a short-stirrup class, the expected outfit consists of beige jodhpurs, short boots, and leather garters, which are sort of like little belts, under your knees. The garters keep your "joddies" from twisting when you ride. Jodhpurs also have straps with button and loop closures that go under your boot soles to keep them from rising up and showing the world your purple socks!

Fashion Tips

- If you have a schooling helmet, you can put a black velvet cover on it to make it look more formal.
- Make sure your jacket is not too tight across your shoulders or chest when you're in jumping position.
- For any class, a judge won't mark you down for "messy hair," but it's important that your "mane" looks neat and tidy. If you have long hair, braid it in one or two braids. If your hair is shorter, pull it back in a ponytail and then keep it under control with a hair net.

Jumping Faults

Faults are penalties the judge gives you when you make mistakes while jumping. In equitation classes, for example, you can receive penalties for poor rider position, wrong diagonals or leads, bad steering, refusals, run-outs, and knocking down poles.

In jumper classes you're given faults if you have a run-out or knock down a pole. You receive three faults for the first stop, six for the second, and you're eliminated after the third. If your horse knocks down a pole, you get four faults. And if you go off course during a jumping round, you're eliminated and must leave the arena. You're also eliminated if you fall off; if that happens, remount and exit the arena.

If you fall off during a hunter or jumper round at a big show, you're eliminated and must leave the ring. If you're competing at a smaller, schooling show, the judge may let you remount and continue round the course. If she thinks your horse looks dangerous though, she might not let you jump any more.

(LEFT) A refusal or run-out will earn you three faults.
(RIGHT) You are eliminated if you fall off during a round.

Walking a Course

Show organizers post diagrams of the courses outside the arena. Spend a few minutes memorizing the course, and then ask a friend to hold your horse so that you can "walk the course." This means you go into the arena on foot with the other competitors and walk the course as if you're jumping it on your horse.

This is when you plan your round. Think about where you will do your courtesy circle — a 20-meter circle where you pick up the trot or canter and establish a steady pace before you head to the first fence.

Look at each fence and figure out which lead you need to be on before and after each fence. Is there a fence that might spook your horse? Perhaps you'll need to use more leg pressure or give your horse an extra kick as you approach it. Count strides between lines and doubles so you know how many strides your horse needs to take to jump steadily.

After you finish your course walk, try to watch a few fellow competitors jump the course to see how many strides they take in the combinations.

Walking a course will help you prepare for your jumping round.

Memorize the course before you enter the arena.

Warming Up

Most shows have a warm-up arena with two or three fences located near the main arena. This is the place where people walk, trot, and canter to warm up their horses and then pop over a few fences to prepare for the course they are about to jump.

You're not supposed to spend all day in the warm-up arena — it's not a place to endlessly school your horse. It is intended for people who are showing in the next hour or so. At big shows, there will be another schooling arena away from the main ring where you can work your horse while you're at the show.

Give yourself about 45 minutes before a class to warm up. The time you need really depends on your horse. He may need less time if he's an experienced jumper and show horse.

It's a good idea to ask your mom or dad or a friend to accompany you to the warm-up arena if you don't have

Jump the practice fences in the warm-up arena before you compete.

a trainer. The fences in the warm-up arena should be set at about the height of the fences that people are jumping in the class that's going on in the show arena. If the fences are set too high for you, ask your helper to lower them. Your helper also can pick up jump poles if they get knocked down.

At big shows, there will be a ring steward to make sure everything is going well in the warm-up arena, but at smaller shows there may be no one monitoring the area. Unfortunately, warm-up arenas can get crazy. Competitors can be rude and cut you off as you aim for a fence. They may come too close to you and your horse. Try to stay calm and focus on the warm-up fences in front of you.

It's a good idea to let the other competitors know which fence you are about to jump so they move out of your way. For example, if you shout, "the oxer!" people should clear the way for you to jump.

Once you've warmed up your horse on the flat, pop over the smallest fence, usually a cross-rail, a few times. Jump it at the trot first and then pick up a canter. If your horse jumps the cross-rail fence nicely, move on to the vertical or spread fences. Ride confidently over these fences. You don't want your horse to know if you feel nervous.

Don't tire out your horse in the warm-up arena. Remember, you shouldn't need more than 45 minutes in there. Your horse needs to be fresh for your class.

Winning Ribbons!

Everyone says that they don't go to shows to win ribbons, but we all know that it's nice to come home with a ribbon or two! Winning a ribbon shows you that you've been doing a good job at home training your horse or pony. Let's take a look at the different ribbon colors.

First place	blue
Second place	red
Third place	yellow
Fourth place	white
Fifth place	pink
Sixth place	green
Seventh place	purple
Eighth place	brown
Ninth place	gray
Tenth place	pale blue

Did you know that in England a ribbon is called a rosette?

Your Round

When it's your turn to enter the arena, pick up the trot or canter, depending on the class. Establish your horse's pace. If he seems a bit lazy, give him a quick bump with your lower legs. If he feels too speedy, sit deeply in the saddle and relax to encourage him to slow down. Keep your legs on him and ride boldly toward the first fence.

If you hesitate or lack energy yourself, he may stop at the first fence. Aim for the middle and ride confidently! As soon as you are over the first fence, look to the next one. Think about how you will steer your horse to it. Give him a little squeeze with your legs to keep him moving forward.

Concentrate on keeping your horse at the same speed all the way around the course. If he's galloping around like he's at the Kentucky Derby, he could get out of control and run out in front of a fence. If he's poking around like a turtle, he may knock down a pole or refuse. After walking the course, or watching other competitors, you will know how many strides there should be between the fences. Slow your horse down or speed him up to reach the correct number of strides.

Keep your hands down, close to his neck, and hold the reins evenly all the way around the course. Push down your heels and sit in the saddle until you are a few strides away from the fence, then get into the jumping position. Grab hold of some mane if you think your horse might take an extra big leap!

After you jump the last fence of a hunter course, do another circle to slow your horse down. If you're competing in a jumper class, remember to gallop past the finish flags. If you're pleased with the way he jumped, rub his neck and say "good boy." Walk him out of the arena and then ride around the show ground for a few minutes to cool him down.

Always look towards your next fence.

Bells and Clocks

In some jumping classes, you must wait for a signal from the judge before you aim for the first fence. The judge usually sits next to the arena in the back of a truck or up in a tower that overlooks the arena. He or she is the one with the clipboard looking at you!

In jumper classes or in the eventing show jumping phase, you must wait for a bell once you've been called to the ring, then salute the judge before picking up the canter. How do you salute the judge? It's easy — simply nod your head in his or her direction and smile!

In hunter classes, you're on your own. There's no start signal. Just do a courtesy circle and begin your course.

In addition to listening for the bell, you need to watch the clock. Cross-rail, trotting pole, beginner rider and horse, hunter, equitation, and short-stirrup jumping classes are not timed, but you will lose points if you plod around the course at a snail's pace. You must trot or canter around the whole course if you want to take home a ribbon. Don't walk part of the course and then trot around the rest.

The judge is the person with the clipboard who is watching your every move!

Handling Problems

If you have problems while jumping your round, don't panic. Slow down, take a deep breath, and think for a second about the best way to work through the problem.

Refusal. If your horse refuses a jump, don't panic or lose your temper. Give him a quick tap with your crop behind your leg to correct him and then circle him away from the fence. Make a small circle — don't go too far away from the fence — and approach the fence again. Use more leg and ride strongly. If you feel him hesitate in front of the fence, give him a couple of kicks with your legs and tap him with the crop behind your leg.

If you are eliminated for three refusals, take your horse to the warm-up arena and jump him over a few fences. Always end on a good note with your horse, not a bad one.

Run-out. If your horse runs out of a fence, gather your reins up if they have become loose. If he ran out

Don't panic or lose your temper if your horse refuses a fence.

to the right, take a firmer hold on the left rein and put your crop in your right hand. Hold the right rein against his neck and press firmly near the girth with your right leg. If he ran out to the left, take a firmer hold on the right rein, put your crop in your left hand, press firmly near the girth with your left leg and then "kick on" toward the fence.

Memory lapse. If you forget your course, don't freak out! Slow down your horse for a few seconds, take a deep breath, and look around. Once you spot the next fence, put your legs on him again and continue on your way.

If you still can't remember the course, look at the judge. She might tell you where the next fence is. But she may eliminate you and ask you to leave the arena. It all depends on how lenient the judge is. At a small show, the judge will probably help you out. At a bigger show, probably not.

Misbehavior. What if your horse misbehaves during a jumping round? If he bucks or rears, it's important to keep him moving forward. If he's really acting crazy, circle him until you get him back in control. Once he's calmed down and behaving himself, you can head to the next fence. If you can't get him back under control, it's time to slow down to a walk and ask the judge if you may be excused. You'll have to work on his issues at home.

If your horse shies at things in the arena, stay calm and ignore the spooking. Pretend it didn't happen and focus on the first fence. Tighten your hold on the reins so your horse can't look around so much. Most horses get used to the show environment after a few shows, so he

Keep calm and focus on the fences while jumping a course.

should spook less and less as he becomes more experienced and more comfortable at shows.

Just don't get flustered and punish him for spooking. After all, the judge may have been looking at her notes and not even seen the spook. The same goes for whinnying. Ignore it.

Tack Problems. What else could go wrong during your round? What if you lose a stirrup? Don't worry — it's not the end of the world. Try to pick the stirrup back up without looking down and maybe the judge won't notice. Even if she does notice, she probably won't mark you down if you pick up your stirrup quickly.

If a piece of your tack, such as a rein or bridle strap, breaks while you're in the arena, it's best to slow down to a walk and ask to be excused. It's too dangerous to continue. If your stirrup leather snaps, however, and you feel confident that you can continue jumping without the stirrup, give it a go. If you've been riding at home without stirrups, it shouldn't be a problem!

It's a good idea to check your tack at least once a week to make sure it is in good condition. If you clean and condition your tack on a regular basis (which you should!), you'll spot weak leather or frayed girth straps. A show arena is not the place to find out that your tack is brittle and about to snap.

Help! I Lost My Stirrup!

You need to be able to pick up a lost stirrup quickly and calmly so you can continue smoothly around the jumping course if you lose a stirrup at a show. Here's a good exercise to practice at home.

Every time you ride, drop one or both of your stirrups and practice finding them without looking down or reaching for the stirrup with your hand. Do this at the walk and trot and see if you can pick up the stirrup in less than three seconds. Once you've mastered this exercise at the walk and trot, try it at the canter.

End of the Day

After you're done showing for the day, it's important to look after your horse before you head home. Make sure he has a hay net to munch on and some water to drink while you groom him from head to toe. If he's done a lot of jumping, you might want to rinse his legs with an invigorating liniment to soothe his sore muscles.

Taking care of your horse gives you time to think about your day. Did you have fun and enjoy the events? Did it go well? Did you win a ribbon or two? Did your horse seem comfortable and cooperative? What things do you need to work on before the next show? If you had a good day — that's wonderful! All of your hard work at home paid off.

If you aren't satisfied with your day, ask yourself why. Maybe you weren't prepared. Maybe you asked your horse to jump fences that were too big. Think about what went wrong and how you can practice those things at home.

If you have a trainer, you and she must come up with a plan to improve your jumping skills before the next show. You might need to jump more courses at home. You might need to set up some spooky jumps at your barn.

You might even need to take a break from jumping in the arena and go on some trail rides. Gallop over some cross-country fences to make jumping more exciting for your horse. You might find that the next show you want to enter is a cross-country jumping event!

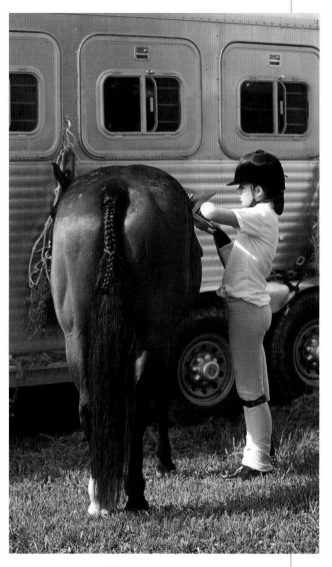

When you're done showing, untack your horse and give him a thorough grooming.

Cross-country Jumping

AS YOU BECOME a more experienced rider, you may find that training in an arena becomes boring for both you and your horse, even if you are jumping regularly. If you're lucky enough to have a cross-country jumping park or farm with schooling fences nearby, you'll probably want to throw open the arena gate and go jumping in wide-open spaces.

Ask your trainer if there's a local park where you can work over fences, and if so, organize a ride there. Some barns may allow you to jump around their private cross-country course for a fee or they may advertise schooling days in local horse publications. Check with riding clubs in your area that may organize schooling days at established courses. Good cross-country courses have jumps for every level. There will be easy 2-foot jumps for beginners and bigger, trickier fences for more experienced riders and horses.

If there's a Pony Club near you, sign up. Jumping cross-country is an important Pony Club activity, and if you're a member, the club will organize outings for you. Also, Pony Clubs are often affiliated with a foxhunt.

Foxhunts take place in the fall and winter and they are a great opportunity to ride with other horses in a group and to jump cross-country-type fences. During a foxhunt, riders follow a group of hounds around the countryside; if a fence or hedge gets in their way, they jump it. The hounds chase the scent of foxes or coyotes. In the olden days, the goal was to catch a fox and kill it. But nowadays, most American hunts just follow the prey and call off the hounds before they catch the fox or coyote.

There are lots of rules when it comes to hunting. You have to wear the correct outfit — formal riding clothes including a helmet, jacket, breeches, gloves, and boots are a must — and you have to act a certain way out on the hunt. No galloping off and jumping by yourself! Ask other people who have hunted to fill you in on all the "dos and don'ts." It can be quite expensive to join a hunt, but kids often hunt for a reduced rate and Pony Clubbers might even hunt for free!

If you don't have much chance to jump out in the open, look in local horse magazines for hunter paces. These are events in which you jump in teams of two or three riders around a cross-country course made up of natural-looking fences. You might jump a stone wall or trot through a creek. Hunter paces are casual events that are lots of fun. They're like fast trail rides with jumps thrown in!

Studs, sometimes called "caulks," are little metal cleats that you screw into predrilled holes in your horse's shoes. They help prevent your horse from slipping on wet or muddy ground.

If you're competing in lower-level cross-country events, you don't need studs. Leave them to horses jumping around huge courses like Rolex Kentucky Three-Day Event!

Your horse must be well behaved on trail rides before you try cross-country jumping.

Outside the Arena

Before you think about jumping outside the arena, you must be a competent jumper inside the arena. You must be able to handle colorful fences that are bigger than the natural ones you intend to jump outside the arena. Your horse must be able to jump a course of fences without being scared by fillers such as flowers, buckets, and brush boxes. He needs to respond immediately to your cues and to be able to concentrate on what he is doing without spooking, shying, or stopping at new sights.

You must also be able to control your horse out on trail rides before you jump outside the arena, and your horse should be experienced going on a variety of trails with different companions. Why? Because horses often become excited when they're in open areas with other horses.

Your quiet, lazy horse could suddenly turn into a speed demon. He may buck or rear when other horses canter by. He may not stop or steer, which is dangerous in a big field, so accustom your horse to trail riding and being ridden with other horses before you jump outside an arena. You and your horse need to be a calm and confident team to safely enjoy the added excitement of jumping cross-country.

Cross-country Fences

Cross-country fences are solid and made of natural-looking materials such as wood and stone. At an event they may be decorated with flowers or other objects. Here are a few of the fences you might see on a course.

BARRELS

DITCH

COOP

BRUSH

BANK

LOG

WATER

HAY

STONE WALL

Schooling over Cross-country Fences

Always jump cross-country fences with an experienced rider or a trainer. Never jump by yourself because if you fall off, you'll have no one to help you. Before you hop on, hike up your stirrups a hole or two — at least one hole shorter than your show jumping length.

Spend 15 to 20 minutes warming up your horse before you jump. Walk, trot, and canter in big circles. Then hand gallop in a big circle and make sure you have control of your horse.

Sometimes horses need to be ridden in a slightly stronger bit when they're galloping in the open. Instead of using a plain snaffle, you might need to grab a snaffle with a twisted mouthpiece or a Kimberwicke. A Kimberwicke is an unjointed metal bit that has a D-shaped ring on each side of the mouthpiece. It also has a curb chain that puts pressure on a horse's jaw when you tug on the reins.

This is a strong bit, because when you lower your hands or pull back, the reins slip down the bit creating a "curb" action. This means the bit pulls down the bridle's sidepieces and puts pressure on the horse's poll area, encouraging him to lower his head and stop pulling against you. You must have gentle hands if you use a Kimberwicke.

You should practice riding in a stronger bit at home before you head out on a cross-country course. Your horse needs to get used to the more severe bit, and you need to learn how to use it properly. Jump a few fences while your horse is wearing the stronger bit and have a gallop around the arena. How much pressure does it take to slow down your horse now? It shouldn't take much.

Now it's time to jump! Find a small, inviting fence, such as a log, to jump a few times. Remember that your horse may be a bit spooky at first, and he may need a strong leg, and even a tap of your crop, to make him go forward.

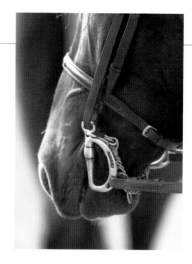

You might need to put a stronger bit, like this Kimberwicke, on your horse when jumping cross-country fences.

Your first cross-country fence should be small and inviting, like this log.

Taking the Jumps

It's important to approach a cross-country fence at a steady pace. Don't tear up to it at a mad gallop because your horse won't be able to jump it properly. As you approach the jump, sit lightly on both seat bones and "wait for the fence." This means sitting quietly and letting your horse figure out where he should take off.

Keep your hands even and steer toward the middle of the obstacle. Push with your legs and seat bones until you're a stride or two away from the fence, then get into jumping position. Release the reins as your horse jumps, move your hands up his neck, and grab onto his mane. When you land on the other side, quietly sit back in the saddle and ride positively away from the fence.

If your horse is nervous about jumping cross-country fences, follow a more experienced horse and rider over the obstacles. Horses don't like being left behind and will often follow another horse over a spooky fence. Make sure you follow from a safe distance — at least three horse lengths apart. You don't want to slam into the other horse's rear end if he refuses in front of you.

Push with your legs and seat bones when you are a stride or two away from the fence.

If your horse is scared of a fence, follow a more experienced horse over the obstacle.

Encourage your horse to leap into water by using your legs and your voice.

Through the Water

One of the most fun things to do when riding cross-country is to jump in and out of water, but some horses get nervous and refuse to enter water. Make sure your horse's first experience is a pleasant one. If he is hesitant, follow another horse into the water. Lean back slightly and encourage him with your legs and voice.

Once he's in the water, walk around and let him have a splash or a drink if he wants. (If he starts splashing a lot, make him move on; some horses like water so much they try to roll in it!) If he's happy, leave the water and then trot or canter him back in.

The first time you try to walk your horse through water, he may try to jump over it. You may be asked to walk, trot, or canter *through* water, or jump down *into* it

during a cross-country event, but you'll never have to jump *over* water. If he tries to jump over water, you could become unbalanced and fall off.

Hold the reins tightly, keep both legs pressed firmly on his sides, and ask him to walk slowly into the water. If he acts like he's going to jump up in the air or try to jump over the water, halt and pat his neck and talk to him until he calms down. Then give him a small squeeze with your calves to ask him to move forward at the walk.

If you can't stop him and he does jump big, loosen your hold on the reins so they slip through your hands. You don't want to jab him in the mouth. Sit back and try to follow his motion over the water. When he lands, shorten up your reins again and ask him to walk. Then turn right around and try walking through the water again. Continue approaching the water slowly until your horse walks through it calmly.

Take It Slow

If your horse is really frightened of water, you'll have to work with him to give him confidence. You may have to hop off and lead him into the water. Never lose your temper or whack him with the crop. He's probably just scared. Be patient and you'll get him in the water. If you have a creek near your house, walk your horse into it every day if possible.

Sometimes in a cross-country event you have to jump down a step into water. Again, follow an experienced horse. If your horse stops at the edge, don't let him turn around. Squeeze with your legs and give him a tap of the crop if needed. The second he leaps in, lean back so you keep your balance. Let the reins slip through your fingers so you don't hurt his mouth. Pick up the reins when you land and ask him to splash forward.

You will never jump *over* water at a cross-country event.

Banks may be jumped going up (above) or down (below).

Jumping a Bank

Some courses have banks to tackle. You may have to jump up or down a bank. If you're jumping up the bank, ride your horse strongly toward the middle and squeeze with both legs. You might have to give him a kick to keep him moving forward. About a stride before the bank, get into jumping position, grab onto his mane, and go with his movement.

When jumping down a bank, slow down but make sure your horse keeps moving at a steady speed. Don't look down at the drop — look ahead into the air. Sit deeply in the saddle and keep your leg on him. As he steps or leaps down, lean back a bit, push down your heels, and loosen your hold on the reins. When he lands, sit back up, pick up your reins, and gallop him to the next fence.

What to Wear

Cross-country riding is more dangerous than trotting around a ring. The fences are solid, they don't fall down like show jumps, and the ground isn't smooth like it is in an arena. There's more of a chance that you or your horse could get hurt, so it's important that both of you wear protective gear. Here's what you need to wear:

- An approved safety helmet
- A snug-fitting, padded safety vest
- Lightweight riding gloves with nonskid palms and fingers
- Breeches or jodhpurs
- Boots

▲ Brushing boots are padded boots that cover a horse's tendon and fetlock area to prevent your horse from kicking himself while galloping. They also protect his lower legs if he knocks a fence. Use them on all four legs.

Overreach or bell boots are stretchy rubber boots that go over your horse's front hooves to protect his pasterns. When galloping, a horse's back hooves reach forward and can cut his pastern area.

▲ Most events require you to wear a special plastic and Velcro armband when you jump that holds a card with your medical details on it. You can buy these armbands at a tack shop.

◀ The dress requirements for dressage and stadium jumping are fairly strict, but during the cross-country jumping phase of eventing, both you and your horse can wear colorful gear. Even purple brushing boots and neon pink helmet covers are allowed!

▶ Some people wear big eventing watches that tell them how fast they're going, but if you're just starting out, it's best to forget about the time and just concentrate on having a safe round.

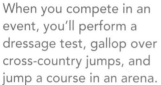

When you compete in an event, you'll perform a dressage test, gallop over cross-country jumps, and jump a course in an arena.

Doing It All — Eventing

If your horse is good on the flat, gallops over cross-country fences, and is comfortable over show jumps, then eventing is the sport for you! Eventing is a true test of your horse's all-round skills. You must perform a dressage test, jump a cross-country course, and then finish with a show jumping, or stadium, round. The cross-country jumping section is the favorite phase for most eventers because it's so exciting.

Try an unaffiliated event for your first competition. Unaffiliated events are not sanctioned by the United States Eventing Association (USEA), so they tend to be smaller, less expensive, and slightly less formal than affiliated shows. Unaffiliated events frequently have smaller jumps that are perfect for new eventers. There is usually a starter division with 2-foot fences, a beginner novice division at 2 foot 6 inches, and a novice division at 2 foot 11 inches. Look in a local horse magazine for advertisements for events.

Walking the Course

When you arrive at a cross-country event, the first thing you must do is pick up your competitor envelope from the show office. This important envelope contains a competitor's number for your dressage and show jumping classes and a pinny, a sturdy paper or plastic vest with a number on it that you slip over your head and wear when you jump cross-country. (If you're given a plastic pinny, remember to return it to the show organizer so they can use it again.) The envelope also has a map of the cross-country course.

Before you tack up your horse, walk the cross-country course with the map several times on foot. If you have a trainer, she should walk around the course with you. You need to know where all the fences are so that you don't get lost. Each fence will be numbered so you don't get confused.

As you "canter" around on foot, look for the flags on every single fence. When you approach a fence, the red flag must always be on your right and the white flag should always be on your left. You'll be disqualified if you jump a fence from the wrong side.

Most competitions assign an optimum time to the course. This is the time in which a rider can complete the course in a safe manner. You want to ride around as close to the optimum time as possible. If you go too quickly, you'll get penalty points. If you go too slowly, you'll also get penalty points.

Divisions of the United States Eventing Association

Competitions that are affiliated with the USEA will contain some or all of these divisions. Check out how high you'll have to jump in each.

Beginner Novice	2 feet 7 inches
Novice	2 feet 11 inches
Training	3 feet 3 inches
Preliminary	3 feet 7 inches
Intermediate	3 feet 11 inches
Advanced	4 feet 1 inch

Three, Two, One, Go!

You'll be given a starting time to jump the cross-country course, so allow yourself enough time in the warm-up area to walk, trot, and canter and to try a few practice fences. Most cross-country rounds begin with the rider in a three-sided starting box. About a minute before your start time, the starter will ask you to walk into the box. Then he'll count down until it's your start time. You must be in the start box when he says "go!"

Start your horse going forward with plenty of energy and head for the first fence. You can trot around a course if you like, but you could get time penalties. As you aim for fence number one, check that the white flag is on your left and the red flag is on the right to make sure you jump the fence from the correct direction.

Three refusals or run-outs at one fence or one refusal or run-out at three different fences means that you're eliminated and you must walk off the course. Each refusal or run-out adds 40 penalty points to your score. And if you fall off your horse at a USEA-sanctioned event, you're eliminated.

If you are eliminated at an event, it's not the end of the world — it just means that you have to go home and practice with your horse. You need to spend more time jumping! Sign up for a few extra lessons with your trainer.

If it's possible, organize a schooling session with your parents or your trainer at the facility where you had problems jumping. Some facilities have schooling days, and you can practice jumping a particular "problem" fence. If you have a local park with cross-country fences, arrange to ride there with your instructor or some horsey pals.

Ride positively around the course, and if you have difficulties with a fence, try to follow a more experienced horse over it. Keep an upbeat attitude and remember to ride strongly when you approach a fence that makes you feel nervous. Don't let your horse know that the fence worries you!

You'll begin the cross-country jumping round in a three-sided start box.

At the End of the Day

Always end your jumping sessions on a good note. If your horse jumps a fence really well and you're pleased with him, give him a pat and let him walk around on a loose rein to cool down. Even if you are struggling on a given day, go back to something your horse does well, like jump a lower fence or even just trot through a few poles, so that your last exercise is a success.

Remember, your horse doesn't know that your goal for the day was to jump that particular combination; he just knows that he is trying to please you and not quite succeeding.

Now that you're becoming a more experienced jumper and you're confident jumping your horse in and out of the arena, have you ever thought about teaching a horse how to jump yourself? Perhaps your trainer has a greenie who is ready to learn how to jump? Or maybe you're thinking of buying a younger, less experienced horse and training him yourself?

Are you up to the challenge? Talk to your parents or your trainer to find out if they think you're ready. In the next chapter we show you a safe and fun way to teach a horse to jump.

Don't let a "problem fence" get you down. Find out if you can school over it later with the help of your trainer.

Teaching Your Horse to Jump

So FAR, WE HAVE MOSTLY dealt with teaching *you* how to jump, but how do horses learn to jump? In this chapter we look at how the skills you've learned in previous chapters can help you to teach your horse to jump.

Jumping comes fairly naturally to horses and ponies. From a very young age, horses are able to leap over obstacles in their way. A foal might bounce over a log in his field, or a stallion might jump over a fence to look for some friendly fillies. But once a horse has a rider on his back, jumping becomes more difficult.

Imagine jumping over a log all by yourself. No problem. But try grabbing your little brother or sister and giving them a piggyback ride over the log. Jumping becomes a little harder, right?

Carrying a passenger affects your balance, and the same goes for a horse with a rider. That's why you must teach a horse gradually to jump with a rider on his back. He needs to learn how to do it slowly, in little steps, so he'll become a confident, capable jumper.

Starting Off

Do you have a horse who doesn't yet know how to jump? Maybe he's a Western pleasure horse and you've decided you'd like to ride him English-style. Maybe he's a young or green horse who has never popped over a fence.

If your horse is healthy, fit, and sound (not lame), there's no reason why he shouldn't be able to jump. Before you begin to jump your horse, though, ask your vet if there is any reason your horse can't jump or any limitations on the amount or type of jumping he can do.

Don't begin teaching your horse to jump until he's at least four years old or even older if he is a slow-maturing breed or a particularly large horse. He can try a tiny log or cross-pole at three years of age, but don't jump him over anything higher or wider.

Even a Western pleasure horse can pop over a fence. It's not very comfortable jumping in a Western saddle though!

A young horse's bones don't finish growing until he's about six years old, and the extra strain and stress of jumping when he's too young can result in an injury or cause him to get arthritis later on in life.

If you haven't jumped with your horse before, ask your parents or trainer if they think he's capable of jumping fences, and if they think you are experienced enough to be his primary trainer. Ask yourself this honest question: Are you a capable, confident rider?

If you are nervous about jumping, it's better to let a more experienced rider teach your horse how to jump. You might even think about sending your horse off to spend a month or two at your trainer's barn so she can teach your horse how to jump. That way your trainer can ride your horse more frequently and he can jump more. Arrange to visit your horse several times a week so you can ride him, too.

If you decide you're ready to take on the training yourself, look around the arena or field where you plan to teach your horse how to jump. All of the fences and poles must be made of safe materials. If your beginner jumper bumps into a jump or knocks down a pole, you don't want the whole fence to fall apart and scare or hurt him.

Before you start teaching your horse how to jump, make sure he has a well-fitting English saddle. Jumping in a Western saddle is uncomfortable for both you and your horse. And stick to the mildest bit possible, such as a snaffle, in case you lose your balance and pull on your horse's mouth.

Teaching a horse to jump should be stress-free if you follow a careful, step-by-step system and take your training very slowly.

Stick to a snaffle bit, like this mild D-ring, when teaching a horse how to jump.

Never jump a horse, especially a horse who is still learning about jumping, without supervision. It's not worth the risk!

Poles are useful for training your horse.

Scatter Some Poles

Start by putting a few poles on the ground around your arena or the area of the field where you school your horse. Incorporate them into your everyday schooling. If you're trotting in a circle, trot over a pole or two. If you're cantering down the long side of the arena, place a pole where you can canter over it easily. But don't get into jumping position when you ride over the poles — you don't want your horse to actually jump over the pole just yet; just walk, trot, or canter over it as if it isn't there.

If your horse leaps the pole, slow him down and walk him over it several times until he goes over it nicely. You don't want him to get overly excited about trotting or cantering over a pole. Stick to riding over poles for a few weeks.

When you're out on trails, walk your horse over small logs so he becomes accustomed to lifting his legs over obstacles. If you have some hills in your field, trot up them and walk down them to strengthen your horse's leg muscles and make him more fit. Your horse needs to be in good shape if he's going to be a great jumper!

Walk your horse over small logs out on the trail.

When your horse is comfortable going over single poles, set up a line of several trotting poles about 5 feet apart. You may have to adjust the distance if your horse knocks the poles or tries to jump several poles at once. Incorporate trotting poles into your daily schooling regime. Walk through the line once or twice so your horse learns to pick up his feet. Then try the line at a trot and approach the exercise from both directions. You can do this while posting or in jumping position. Practice over the trotting poles for a week or two.

Practice over trotting poles for a few weeks before you actually jump your horse.

Your horse's first small jump should be set up at the end of a line of trotting poles.

First Jump

When your horse can trot over the line of poles consistently and confidently, add a small cross-rail fence, about a foot off the ground and about 9 feet away from the last trotting pole. Get into jumping position and aim your horse at the middle of the fence as you trot through the line of poles.

Your horse should already be picking up his feet and concentrating on the poles, so a tiny fence sneaking up on him at the end shouldn't faze him. If he has problems jumping the fence, you may have to adjust the distance between the last pole and the fence.

Remember to stay in jumping position and put your hands slightly up his neck so you loosen the reins a little. Green horses often jump big, and you don't want to get left behind and yank on his mouth. Grab hold of some mane or a neck strap every time you head for a fence.

If your horse canters in front of the fence, that's okay. Just let him go forward at the canter and bring him back to a trot after the fence. Keep him moving forward the second he lands. Think "forward" every time you jump!

If your horse is trotting smoothly over the poles, a tiny fence at the end of the line should be easy for him to jump.

Always head in alternate directions after you land. Turn right after you jump and then the next time over the poles and the fence, turn left. Go straight sometimes and ask your horse to halt from the trot. You want him to learn that he can go in any direction after a jump and that you are the one who tells him what to do next.

Once your horse has mastered the cross-rail fence at the end of the trotting poles, ask your helper to make the fence a small upright. This means the poles go straight across instead of crossing in the middle. It should be only 12 to 18 inches high. Place a ground pole 3 to 5 inches in front of the fence; this fills the fence in and makes it easier for your horse to jump. Your horse should be used to jumping a fence at the end of the poles, so jumping an upright fence should be easy for him.

As you head down the line of poles, stay in jumping position, push your hands slightly forward so you loosen the reins, and look straight ahead over the fence. Your horse should be moving forward at an energetic pace, and he should pop over it nicely.

Small Upright Fence

Now your horse must learn to jump without trotting poles. Set up a small upright fence, no larger than 18 inches, with a ground pole directly in front of it.

- Trot your horse around the arena until he's going forward in a balanced way.

- Give yourself plenty of room to aim straight at the fence. Look up, over the fence, not down!

- Get into jumping position a few feet away from the fence and loosen the reins slightly by pushing your hands forward.

- Aim for the middle of the fence. Your horse should leap over it without a problem. When he lands, sit back and send him forward with your legs.

- Remember to give him a pat and to praise him if he jumps nicely.

Jump the fence from both directions. Once your horse is comfortable jumping at the trot, try a canter. If he starts rushing or acting silly, go back to the trot. If he still rushes at the trot, you need to go back to practicing your flat work.

Do lots of transitions to get your horse to listen to you, and once he's behaving again, try trotting and cantering over poles. Once he's calm and obedient, you can try trotting, then cantering, over the upright.

Always look up, over the fence, not down!

Lead your horse over fences to build up his confidence. You'll have to be fit though!

Follow the Leader

Here's another way to help your horse become a confident jumper. Place a few poles on the ground and set up a few small jumps in the arena. Put on your helmet and a pair of gloves, and outfit your horse with a halter and lead rope. Lead him around the arena a few times so he gets a look at the fences.

Walk and trot around the arena on foot — this will help you get fitter, too! After about 10 minutes of warming up, guide him on a loose lead rope over a pole or two at the trot. If he follows you nicely, you can leap over a fence. He should follow you. Jump the other fences, too. This exercise teaches your horse to jump without having a rider on his back, so there's no chance of making him unbalanced. And it's fun!

Lead your horse like this at least once a week while he's learning how to jump. You can raise the fences as he grows more confident. If your horse trusts you, he'll jump most things to keep up with you. Keep a few treats in your pocket and reward him when he jumps well.

As you raise the fences, you might not be able to jump them yourself. Simply run alongside each fence and raise your hand so the lead rope goes over the jump standard and doesn't get caught. Using barrels as standards is a good idea for this exercise, because they aren't very tall. You can also lead your horse over small cross-country fences.

Ground Work

Before you try leading your horse over jumps, it's important that he be easy to work with on the ground. You should be able to lead him without being run over or pulled all over the place.

Teach your horse voice commands while working with him on the ground. He should learn that "whoa" means slow down and that "tee-rot" or a clucking sound means speed up.

Practice some ground work with your horse, before you try jumping him in-hand.

Green horses often jump BIG over a fence!

Adding Fences

After a few jumping sessions, your horse should be jumping the upright fence with confidence. Now you can set up an easy course of five or six fences. Design a small course and go through it at the trot.

Don't worry if your horse jumps big or awkwardly. Remember, he's just learning how to jump! Jump your course two or three times at the trot and give him a pat after the final fence. Don't overdo your practice sessions, and always end on a positive note.

After a few weeks of practicing at the trot, try cantering around the course. If your horse lands on the wrong lead after a fence, slow him down to a trot and ask for the correct lead.

Keep the jumps at 18 to 24 inches for the first several months of training. Never rush your green horse by asking him to jump huge fences before he's ready. Ask your instructor when she thinks that you and your horse are ready to tackle bigger fences.

Jumping Small Grids

Doing grids is a great way to build up your green jumper's confidence. Grids make your horse more agile and teach him how to look after himself when jumping. Most horses find grids, especially small ones, quite easy and are happy to jump in and out of them.

Set up a small grid (see chapter three). The first few times you jump it, leave all the poles on the ground so the grid is simply made of trotting poles. Then raise the poles of the last fence to make a small cross-rail.

Eventually you can raise the middle fence and finally the first fence, so that your horse is jumping three in a row. If you build the grid gradually, your horse should jump through happily.

Start by trotting your horse into the grid, but if he picks up a canter on the way through, let him canter. The most important thing is to keep him moving forward through a grid. Bring him back to a trot once you finish the grid.

If your horse has trouble more than once going through a grid, and is stumbling or knocking over poles, you probably need to adjust the spacing between the fences to fit his stride.

Don't try to jump a pony through a grid set up for a horse (or vice versa). It just won't work. Your pony or horse will get frustrated, and he might refuse to jump.

You can play around with the height of the fences in the grid, but the last fence should always be the same height or bigger than the first two. Don't start out with a big first fence and end with a tiny one.

Try an easy pole course at your horse's first jumping show.

Your First Jumping Show

Once your horse is jumping small fences at home, you can take him to a show. Start out by doing a pole course or a cross-rail course at your first show. Don't enter a class with higher fences than you're schooling at home, because you may overface your horse and ruin his confidence. Stick to small fences at first, and you're sure to come home with a happy horse, and perhaps a ribbon or two!

Going to a show is a great way to see how your training has worked. If your horse behaves himself and jumps everything in front of him, you've done a great job with him back at the barn. If he doesn't shine at a show, you must figure out where things went wrong and decide what you need to focus on at home. Keep a positive attitude and work hard with your horse — you'll be jumping clear rounds before long!

With practice, you'll soon be jumping lots of different fences.

Jumping into the Future!

Now that you've read this book cover to cover, it's time to go out and jump some fences! But don't toss this book on a shelf and let it get dusty. Keep it in the tack room or in your grooming box so you can refer to it from time to time. You might need to practice a jumping exercise that we've shown you or you might want to set up one of our fun jumping courses in your own arena. Use this book as a reference tool to help you improve your jumping skills or solve jumping problems that crop up.

Once you start jumping, you'll soon discover that it's addictive! You'll never want to stop. And because riding is an activity that all ages can enjoy, you may be jumping far into the future. So fasten your chinstrap and raise your stirrups a hole or two. Ask your horse to pick up a nice, bouncy canter and point him at the oxer ahead of you. See you on the other side of the fence!

Jumping is a blast!

INDEX

Page numbers in *italic* indicate illustrations; those in **bold** indicate tables.

thighs and jumping position, 8, *8, 11, 13*
timed events, 83, 91, 109, 110
tires, cross-country jump, 74, *74*
trailer loading, 80
trail riding and
    cross-country jumping, 99, *99*
    teaching your horse to jump, 116, *116*
trainers (instructors)
    finding good, viii–x, 3–5
    teaching your horse to jump, 115
training division (USEA), **109**
transitions, 120
trip, defined, 80
triples, 34
trotting
    lines, 27, *27*
    small course, 28, *28*
trotting pole classes, 81, 91
trotting poles
    exercise, 37–39, *37–39*
    flatwork, 3, *3,* 13–15, *13–15*
    teaching your horse to jump, 116–17, *116–19,* 118, 119
two-point position. *See* jumping position

U

unaffiliated events, cross-country jumping, 108
United States Eventing Association (USEA), ix, 108, **109**
upper body and jumping position, 8, *8, 11, 13*
upright fence (small), 118, *118–20,* 119, 120

V

verticals
    grids, 44, *44,* 47, *47*
    jump, your first, 18, *18,* 21, *21*
vest (safety), 5, 6, *6*
veterinary checkup, 52, *52,* 53

W

"waiting for the fence," 102, *102*

walking a course
    cross-country jumping, 97, 109
    jump, your first, *31,* 31–32, **32**
    show, jumping at a, 87, *87*
warming up
    cross-country jumping, 101
    show, jumping at a, *88,* 88–89
warm-up classes, 83
watches, cross-country, 107, *107*
watching classes before showing, 81, 84, 87, 90
water jumps (Liverpool)
    building, 72, *72*
    cross-country jumping, *100, 103,* 103–4
Western pleasure horses and jumping, 114, *114*
"wings." *See* standards
winning ribbons, 89, **89,** *89*

Recommended Reading

Allen, Linda J. *101 Jumping Exercises for Horse & Rider* (Storey Publishing, 2002)

Haas, Jessie. *Safe Horse, Safe Rider: A Young Rider's Guide to Responsible Horsekeeping* (Storey Publishing, 1994)

Harris, Susan. *The United States Pony Club Manual of Horsemanship* (John Wiley & Sons Canada, Ltd., 1994)

Hill, Cherry. *Horse Care for Kids* (Storey Publishing, 2002)

Hill, Cherry. *Horse Health Care: A Step-by-Step Photographic Guide to Mastering Over 100 Horsekeeping Skills* (Storey Publishing, 1997)

Hill, Cherry. *How to Think Like a Horse* (Storey Publishing, 2006)

Hill, Cherry. *101 Arena Exercises: A Ringside Guide for Horse & Rider* (Storey Publishing, 1995)

Richter, Judy. *Riding for Kids* (Storey Publishing, 2003)

Storey's Horse-Lover's Encyclopedia, edited by Deborah Burns. (Storey Publishing, 2001)

Ward, Lesley. *English Riding, 2nd Edition* (BowTie Press, 2004)

Ward, Lesley. *Let's Go to a Show: How to Win Ribbons & Have Lots of Fun Too!* (BowTie Press, 2002)

Ward, Lesley. *Your Healthy and Happy Horse: How to Care for Your Horse & Have Fun Too!* (BowTie Press, 2003)